D0852172

WILLIAM

WILLIAM

HRH Prince William of Wales

Tim Graham and Peter Archer

SIMON &
SCHUSTER

First published in Great Britain by Simon & Schuster UK Ltd, 2003
A Viacom Company
Copyright © Tim Graham and Peter Archer, 2003
This book is copyright under the Berne Convention.
No reproduction without permission. All rights reserved.
The right of Tim Graham and Peter Archer to be identified as authors of this work has been asserted
in accordance with sections 77 and 78 of the Copyright, Designs and Patents Act, 1988.
1 3 5 7 9 10 8 6 4 2
Simon & Schuster UK Ltd Africa House 64–78 Kingsway London WC2B 6AH
www.simonsays.co.uk
Simon & Schuster Australia Sydney
A CIP catalogue record for this book is available from the British Library
ISBN 0 7432 3986 5 (Hardback)
ISBN 0 7432 4857 0 (Paperback)
Designed by the Senate
Printed and bound in Great Britain by Butler & Tanner, Frome, Somerset

WILLIAM

INTRODUCTION

He has inherited his mother's good looks and his father's intellect. Rich, handsome and charming, he is arguably the most eligible bachelor in the world. He is a pin-up and a role model. He is a dutiful son and grandson, a loving brother and friend. He is his mother's enduring legacy and his father's pride and joy.

Prince William is a dashing young man destined to be king. Second in line to the throne of Great Britain and Northern Ireland, he is the monarchy's future and its great hope.

The most popular member of the Royal Family, William has charisma and a flirtatious wit. His youth, athletic physique and engaging smile make girls swoon. But he is also respected for his strength of character and the way he conducted himself in adversity after his mother's early and cruel death.

Young and old cannot resist his style and impeccable manners. Firm of handshake and quick to chat, he can put people at ease, combining the right measure of curiosity, humour and compassion.

In many ways, William breaks the mould. He is a modern prince in touch with his contemporaries in a fast-changing world. To the credit of his mother and father, he has been brought up in the real world. Of course, he was born into immense wealth and privilege. He has had the best that money can buy. But his humility is intact. Due largely to the efforts of Diana, Princess of Wales, he was shown how the less fortunate, the homeless and the sick, live and suffer. Diana was determined that, if she were to be the People's Princess, her son and heir would be the People's Prince. She showed William how to have fun too and what it was like to live a 'normal' life. With younger brother Prince Harry, they dressed in jeans and baseball caps, went to the cinema or an amusement park and ate fast food.

The Prince of Wales has taught his son the importance of heritage and tradition. William was born to be king. He has inherited his father's destiny. He may have been frightened by the high expectation and weight of duty on his young shoulders, but the gentle encouragement and coaching of his father have stood him in good stead. The ways of the Windsors were not always to the liking of Diana but, no matter how much he resembles the Princess,

William is also his father's son.

Charles's strong sense of social justice and the help he gives to the needy, particularly disadvantaged youngsters through his widely acclaimed Prince's Trust charity, have helped fashion the way William sees the world. His father's devotion to duty, as heir to the throne, has also set William an example to follow. In public, Charles may not be a 'touchy-feely' parent, as Diana was, but in private he is always loving, caring and affectionate. A grateful William returns the love shown to him by his father and he admires his achievements.

Just as William follows in his mother's wake as a champion swimmer, he emulates his father's sporting prowess on the polo field. Despite Diana's dislike of such things, William hunts and shoots in the way of royalty and country folk. He shares Charles's love of the countryside and his interest in promoting a sustainable environment.

As William turns twenty-one, on 21 June 2003, he presents himself as a truly remarkable young man who has experienced different ways of life and travelled much of the world. Well-educated at Eton and now at St Andrews University in Scotland, he is already an accomplished individual, living up to his early promise.

It would appear that William has turned out exceptionally well despite a childhood scarred by his parents' highly publicised marriage breakdown and bitter divorce. Who could possibly imagine the utter devastation he felt, at the tender age of fifteen, when his mother was fatally injured in a Paris car crash? Only time will tell if William survived these harrowing experiences without serious and lasting emotional harm. If he is unscathed by his troubled upbringing, it is surely a testament to the love his parents poured on him, despite their harmful quarrelling.

Young people in Britain are growing up in a baffling, complex and rapidly changing world, where divorce rates are increasing and traditional institutions are breaking down. William's story represents the strains of modern life and it is perhaps because of this that young people identify closely with him. Pollsters report that youngsters consider William to be the Royal to modernise the monarchy as a new-style head of state in tune with the twenty-first century. Even if the monarchy were abolished, William

would still be one of the favourites to become president of the new republic of Great Britain.

Many youngsters want William to usurp his father and be king instead of him. But that could never be, nor is it something William would want. Modest and unassuming, when others in his position could show unbearable arrogance, he is supportive of his father and his number-one fan.

An indication of William's popularity is that his mere presence in Scotland, where he is now an undergraduate, is said by some political commentators to have put back any serious threat of republicanism by at least fifty years. This is much to live up to for a young man but, even if it is true, William is clearly a future leader who will have to face a growing questioning of traditional institutions, including the monarchy.

Such immense pressures are at odds with William's honest desire to be simply an ordinary young man. At present, the tall, blond, blue-eyed student prince is struggling against intense media interest to preserve a private life of his own. He asks to be called William – not Your Royal Highness, Sir or even Prince William. He wants to be accepted for what he is and not who he is. He is willing to be just one of the crowd and a team player. But he shows promise as a leader and a mediator. For whatever reasons, he is seeking the approval of his peers. William wants to be liked – and is adored.

Wearing the student uniform of jeans and trainers, his hair carefully tousled, William has assumed the identity of an undergraduate in Scotland's oldest seat of learning, St Andrews. Sharing a comfortable flat with a friend from Eton and an attractive brunette, not to mention his police bodyguard, William is enjoying a degree more independence than his days at boarding school allowed him. Geared up with a car and a mountain bike, William intends to enjoy his student years and to have fun in the university town with a reputation for partying. But he knows the eyes of the world are on him and that if – or when – he slips up, his mistakes will be magnified, such is the nature of the public scrutiny he attracts. His story is a compelling tale of our times.

1

BORN TO BE KING

William's story begins before he was born. It was a
beginning that, told through the world's media, had all
the drama of a royal soap opera, a media production
delivered in cliff-hanging episodes. Seen in another way,
however, it reveals much about the life – both private and
public – into which he was born. By looking at it this way,
we can begin to try to understand who William is and who
he may become.

By the late 1970s, his father, the Prince of Wales, was
under pressure to find a bride and secure the line of
succession to his future throne. In his youth Charles had
dallied with suitable, mainly aristocratic, girls but had lost
the love of his bachelor days. An older woman captivated
him and would remain a potent force in his life. However,
Camilla Shand was to marry another man.

Charles's own childhood had been a difficult one,
growing up in the glare of publicity with almost every
decision made for him as the heir to the throne. He disliked
his senior school, Gordonstoun in Scotland, the choice of
his amiably quizzical and exacting father, the Duke of
Edinburgh. He craved the attention of his mother but, for
most of his young life, she held down a demanding and full-
time job as Queen and Head of the Commonwealth. She
pledged herself to a lifetime of duty and work necessarily
came before play.

Charles reached his thirties still a bachelor. Time
seemed to be running out for him to find the right girl to
marry. She would have to be attractive, kind, from a good
background and, of course, able to bear healthy children.
She could not have a past love life of any serious nature.
There could be no skeletons in the cupboard that could
later prove an embarrassment to the Royal Family.
Whoever and wherever she was, Charles's bride had to be
untainted and innocent.

Lady Diana Spencer, almost thirteen years Charles's
junior, was born at Park House, on the Queen's
Sandringham estate in Norfolk. Her marital credentials
could not be faulted. Lady Diana's father had inherited the
family earldom and stately home, Althorp, in
Northamptonshire, and she was still young enough not to
have had a serious boyfriend.

But Diana came from a broken home. At the age of six
she faced the trauma of her mother walking away from a

Diana beamed a broad smile, content that she had done what was required of her and produced a male heir to the throne.

failing marriage. Her father fought an acrimonious legal battle to win custody of his four children and later married Raine, Countess of Dartmouth, daughter of the romantic novelist Barbara Cartland. Diana and the other children clashed with their stepmother and referred to her as 'Acid Rain'.

Charles first dated Lady Diana's elder sister, Sarah. However, in 1980 his eyes were opened to Diana and romance blossomed, although up to their formal engagement, which was announced on 24 February 1981, she had been required, by Royal protocol, to call her royal suitor 'Sir'!

The fairy-tale wedding, in London's St Paul's Cathedral, on 29 July 1981, was watched on television by a staggering 750 million people worldwide. With Britain in the grips of rising unemployment and industrial strife, the splendour of the royal occasion offered pure escapism.

The twenty-year-old Diana Spencer became Princess of Wales and was catapulted, almost overnight, from relative obscurity to megastardom. She soon became the most-photographed woman in the world. How could she possibly cope?

On 5 November 1981, Buckingham Palace announced that the Princess of Wales was expecting her first child. Amid the media flurry there was plentiful speculation on whether Diana's baby would be a male heir. The birth of the Prince and Princess of Wales's child would not simply be a matter of their personal happiness, it would be a great national event.

Parents-to-be Charles and Diana poured over books on childbirth and parenting, and mused over names for a boy or a girl, but without agreement. Charles even went to an ante-natal class while Diana delighted in wearing designer maternity dresses. A routine scan revealed a normal healthy baby and the Prince and Princess were told it was a boy.

For much of her pregnancy Diana stayed at Buckingham Palace while the couple's new London home, Apartments 8 and 9 at Kensington Palace, were renovated and the nursery prepared. It was not until five weeks before the baby's birth that they actually moved in. By then Diana was feeling the strain of the constant media interest in her condition and there were already pressures building up within her marriage.

When Diana was three months' pregnant, she was suffering morning sickness and felt thoroughly wretched. She was having difficulty coming to terms with her new status and celebrity, and felt her husband was unsympathetic to her plight. Unknown to the Princess, the Queen had summoned Fleet Street editors to the Palace where her press secretary had requested a degree of privacy for Diana. But the royal pregnancy sold newspapers and there was little let up.

During this sensitive time for the unborn child, Diana made a desperate cry for help and, in January 1982 while at Sandringham, she threatened to take her own life. Charles thought she was crying wolf but a distraught Diana threw herself down a flight of stairs. Fortunately, she was not seriously hurt and the baby was unharmed. Even before his birth, William was resilient and a survivor.

Prince William was born at 9.03 p.m. in the private Lindo Wing of St Mary's Hospital, Paddington, west London, on Monday 21 June 1982. Notice of the royal birth was posted on the forecourt railings of Buckingham Palace in the traditional manner. Congratulatory messages and gifts poured into the Palace from world leaders, foreign royal families and many hundreds of ordinary people.

According to genealogists, William was born the most British heir to the throne since King James I. If he succeeds Charles as king he will be the sixty-third monarch of England since Egbert of Wessex and the forty-fourth since the Norman Conquest of 1066. He is likely to call himself King William V, although he could assume another name as king in the same way as his great-grandfather, for example, who was christened Albert but crowned King George VI.

William was the first royal baby so close to the throne to be born in hospital rather than a palace. The Prince of Wales was present at the birth which, in the end, was without serious complications. For some sixteen hours of labour, Diana struggled to give birth. She was continually sick and her temperature soared. At one point royal gynaecologist Mr – later Sir – George Pinker considered performing an emergency Caesarean operation. But, with the aid of an epidural injection in the base of her spine, Diana was eventually able to give birth without resorting to forceps or a Caesarean. William weighed in at a healthy 7lbs

1oz and nurses put a band around his tiny wrist labelling him 'Baby Wales'.

Two hours later, Charles emerged from the hospital and spoke to the waiting reporters. 'Is the baby like you, Sir?' one asked. Charles chuckled and replied, 'Fortunately, no.' He revealed that his new-born son had 'a wisp of fair hair, blondish, with blue eyes'. Witnessing the birth had been an overwhelming experience and 'a very adult thing to do,' he said.

Without delay, the Queen visited the hospital to see the baby boy who was second in line to her throne. 'I'm delighted,' she said. William's maternal grandmother, Frances Shand-Kydd, visiting with Diana's sister Jane Fellowes, exclaimed, 'He's lovely. There's so much happiness.' Diana's father, Earl Spencer, said, 'He's the most beautiful baby I've seen.'

The rest of the world saw William when, the next day at 6 p.m., Charles's and Diana emerged from the hospital with their baby. As the camera shutters clicked into action, it was the beginning of the little Prince's life of being photographed. The couple whose fairy-tale wedding had been watched on television by millions around the globe were again the centre of world attention – this time with William. The baby slept peacefully in Charles's arms, wrapped in a white lace shawl, while Diana beamed a broad smile, content that she had done what was required of her and produced a male heir to the throne.

For the readers of horoscopes, William was born under the sign of Cancer – the crab. Astrologers claimed he was born on an auspicious day, the day of an eclipse, and attributed to him the characteristics of a leader, combining traits of inspiration and tenacity, courage with respect for tradition. The newborn Prince would be sensitive, protective, cautious, shrewd, conservative and would respect family life. William's chart also showed he would grow to be a fine all-round sportsman and scholar, with indications of an extremely active and fertile mind. He would be both quick-witted and humorous, and would probably entertain his family from an early age with his ability to act the clown.

Gynaecologist Mr Pinker and four nurses who helped at the birth were among the guests at William's christening in the grand Music Room at Buckingham Palace. Charles had

favoured the name Arthur for his first son and Albert, after Queen Victoria's consort, for his second. But Diana triumphed in the battle of the names with her choice and, with a hint of compromise, the baby was christened William Arthur Philip Louis.

The baptism, performed with water from the River Jordan by Archbishop of Canterbury Dr Robert Runcie, took place on 4 August 1982, the Queen Mother's eighty-second birthday. The royal matriarch was present to hear her great-grandson howl after the ceremony as photographs were being taken. 'He certainly has a good pair of lungs,' she remarked. Meanwhile Diana soothed William, who was dressed in the Victorian royal christening robe of Honiton lace over a satin petticoat, by letting him suck her little finger.

Charles's wishes seemed to override Diana's when it came to choosing William's godparents. As is customary with members of the Royal Family, more than two were selected. They were ex-King Constantine of Greece, known to the Royal Family as Tino; philosopher and the Prince of Wales's mystical mentor, Sir Laurens van der Post; Lord Romsey, grandson of Charles's greatest influence, Earl Mountbatten of Burma; Princess Alexandra, a popular member of the Royal Family; the Duchess of Westminster, the wife of Charles's good friend and wealthiest landowner in England, the Duke of Westminster; and Lady Susan Hussey, the Queen's senior lady-in-waiting.

With the possible exception of Sir Laurens van der Post, William's godparents reflected the Royal Family's preference for safe, solid members of the 'Establishment'. Sir Laurens, however, was chosen to impart a philosophical and spiritual dimension to William's life, a way of thinking much appreciated by Charles but less valued by Diana. But the philosopher's death during William's adolescence limited his influence on the young Royal's development. King Constantine, an ebullient character, is a strong influence and also a link with the homeland of William's paternal grandfather, Prince Philip. The choice of Lord Romsey reflects the enduring power of the Mountbattens within the Windsor dynasty.

Life was soon eventful for William who, even before his first birthday, had travelled abroad with his parents. At just nine months old, he accompanied the Prince and Princess of Wales on their official visit to Australia and New Zealand in early 1983. Diana, who could not bear the thought of leaving William behind, broke with royal tradition and took her baby boy on the six-week tour. The decision was made easier when Australian Prime Minister Malcolm Fraser wrote to the royal couple inviting them to bring their son. It was an unprecedented trip for a royal baby.

William stole the hearts of Australians who nicknamed him 'Billy the Kid'. He was too young to travel everywhere with his parents and stayed with nanny Barbara Barnes at Woomargama, a remote 4,000-acre sheep station in New South Wales. Charles and Diana returned as often as they could to see him there. But even the short periods away from her son were difficult for the Princess to bear. In Canberra, when a young mother told Diana she envied her, the Princess replied, 'Oh no, I envy you. I wish I could stay home with my baby.'

In New Zealand, the baby Prince went on a royal 'crawlabout' when his mother and father presented him to the world's media for an official photocall. William, dressed in a smocked, embroidered silk romper suit, was positioned on a rug between his parents on the lawn of Government House in Auckland when suddenly he took off, at the double, on all fours. Later Diana helped him to stand up on his shaky legs for the first time in public. At the end of the photo session, Diana whispered in his ear, 'Who's a little superstar, then?'

William's progress since birth had been recorded by his mother and father. His first smile was at six weeks. He could roll onto his tummy and support his upper body on his forearms at seventeen weeks. He could sit with support at six months and without help shortly afterwards. He had his first teeth at eight months and was to start walking at fourteen months. Describing William at just a few weeks old, the Prince of Wales said, 'He gets noisier and angrier by the day.'

In particular, the proud parents liked to surround themselves with photographs of their first-born. Pictures from photo sessions with media photographers were as much for Charles and Diana's use and enjoyment as they

were for publication in newspapers and magazines. One such photograph, taken in February 1983 in the living room at the Waleses' Kensington Palace apartment, was used for William's first passport.

Barbara Barnes helped to look after William for the first four years of his life. Diana was impressed with Miss Barnes who, for fourteen years, had cared for the four children of Princess Margaret's friends, Lord and Lady Glenconner. Nanny Barnes was assisted by Mrs Olga Powell. Although she employed nannies, Diana made it clear that she would be closely involved in William's upbringing. She was determined that he would be showered with the hugs and kisses which she felt had been missing from her own childhood.

Nanny Barnes, a forest worker's daughter, had no formal training – she simply loved children. She did not wear a uniform and preferred to be called by her first name, although William was to call her 'Ba-Ba'. On her appointment, she said, 'I do not see any different problems in bringing up a royal baby. I treat all children as individuals. I am not a graduate of any sort of nannies' college. I have accumulated my knowledge from many years of experience with children.' During her time with the Waleses, Nanny Barnes developed a close relationship with William, but in his early years he proved a handful. He was a royal terror who was probably being over-indulged.

In June 1983, Charles and Diana were on tour again, this time in Canada and without William. The trip lasted only two weeks but coincided with his first birthday. The royal couple telephoned to wish William a happy birthday and were rewarded with what Charles called 'a few little squeaks'. During a walkabout in Ottawa, the Canadian capital, Diana told a royal fan, 'I really am missing him. He's a beautiful little boy and we are both extremely proud of him.' The Prince of Wales's first Father's Day also occurred during the Canadian tour and he received a card from home showing a magician pulling a rabbit out of a hat and bearing the message, 'Dad, I think you're magic.'

Though William did not, of course, write the card himself, he was turning out to be a precocious little boy. And his natural curiosity increasingly landed him in trouble. Yet his father loved his mischief-making and nicknamed him 'Wombat' after the curious Australian

mammal. It is unlikely, however, that the Prince of Wales found William's prank of trying to flush a pair of Papa's shoes down the toilet very endearing. Then there was the time when, at the age of fifteen months, the inquisitive toddler Prince pressed a button on the nursery wall at Balmoral, which sent Scottish police cars scrambling to seal off the royal estate.

Just before Christmas 1983, photographers were invited to Kensington Palace for a Prince William photo shoot. The star of the show toddled into the walled garden of the Palace, standing 2ft 10ins tall and with eleven teeth. He also showed off his vocabulary when his mother pointed to the sky and asked, 'What's that?' William looked up at the noisy aircraft and said, 'Helicopter.' Diana had dressed William in a snug, navy-blue snowsuit for the Christmas photocall and, after pictures appeared on newspaper front pages, stores throughout the country sold out of similar suits. The Prince of Wales said of his son and heir, 'William is a splendid little character and very good-natured. He seems to have quite a good sense of humour and he is very outgoing.' The Princess said, 'He is not at all shy but very polite.'

Following a Christmas spent at Windsor Castle, Buckingham Palace announced the Princess of Wales was pregnant with her second child and that the birth was expected in September.

But before the new arrival came on the scene, William starred in another photocall, this time to mark his second birthday. He stepped out in blue dungaree-shorts and matching striped T-shirt for a game of football in the Kensington Palace garden. Charles played in the mini royal kickabout while a pregnant Diana looked on. Ever curious, William spotted a TV camera and ran over to investigate. 'He's really interested in cameras,' said his father, as William peered into the viewfinder for an action replay of his soccer skills. 'What's that?' William asked, pointing to the soundman's boom. 'It's a microphone,' explained Charles, 'a big sausage that picks up everything you say — and you are starting early!'

That year, stargazers predicted William would grow to 6ft 2ins, would marry between the ages of twenty-six and twenty-nine, and would re-marry after an emotional upheaval in his early forties.

A brother for William was born on 15 September 1984. Prince Henry Charles Albert David of Wales was to be known as Prince Harry. On the morning after the birth, William was taken to St Mary's Hospital to see his baby brother. On the steps of the hospital William gave his first public royal wave and had obviously learnt well, moving his uplifted hand as if unscrewing a light bulb. The brotherly encounter in Diana's private room was the beginning of a friendship that would see both boys through trying times in later life.

Harry's christening at St George's Chapel, Windsor, on 21 December that year, showed just how boisterous William had become. The Queen could not distract or restrain him and he ran through the royal gathering like a mini whirlwind until Diana eventually managed to tame her little terror by hugging him so tightly he could not escape.

There were similar toddler tantrums shortly afterwards when Charles and Diana were invited to the Queen Mother's Highland retreat, Birkhall, on the Balmoral estate. William caused havoc in his great-grandmother's dining room and was disrespectful to royal servants. Stories emerged of William shouting at staff, 'When I'm King, I'm going to send all my knights around to kill you.'

The time had come to try to instil some discipline and, despite his father's initial reservations, Diana arranged for William to go to a nursery school. At first Charles had wanted his elder son to be educated at home by a governess in the early years, as he and countless generations of royal children had been before him. But both parents came round to thinking that William needed to interact with other youngsters to develop social skills and, hopefully, calm down.

'William is a splendid little character and very good-natured. He seems to have quite a good sense of humour and he is very outgoing.'

Prince of Wales, November 1983

3

LESSONS TO BE LEARNT

At the age of three, on 24 September 1985, William started at Mrs Mynors' Nursery School, run by Mrs Jane Mynors, in Notting Hill Gate, West London.

He arrived by car at 9.45 a.m. with the Prince and Princess of Wales, and was greeted by the inevitable massed ranks of reporters and photographers, eager to record his first day at school. Fleet Street editors had been informed a week earlier that the young Prince was starting at the nursery. Charles and Diana decided to give the media their full co-operation on the first day, in the hope that journalists would then leave William alone. As Charles's father, the Duke of Edinburgh, once said, living life as a Royal was 'like living in a goldfish bowl'. William's parents knew the feeling and wanted to protect him for as long as they could.

An insistent young Prince had chosen his own outfit for the photocall and wore red shorts, a red check shirt, multicoloured striped jumper and red shoes. 'He was just so excited by it all,' said Diana. 'He was so organised that he chose his own shorts and shirt. It's best to let him do that if you want him to smile at the cameras!'

William's first school reports showed him to be a thoughtful and talented boy. His sporting prowess was documented alongside his artistic achievements in school plays and concerts, although in later years he was embarrassed by his acting and singing at school.

Teachers credited him with a kind and likeable nature. He had a sense of fun and was popular with other children, although he remained somewhat boisterous, earning the nickname 'Basher'. Accompanied everywhere by his police bodyguard, William would tell other children, 'If you don't do what I want, I'll have you arrested.' It was a long way from the diplomatic and self-effacing teenage William who wanted to fit in with the crowd as plain Wills!

The toddler Prince was showing signs that he was being spoilt by Charles and Diana whose over-indulgence or over-identification with their first-born son may have been a consequence of an unsatisfactory marriage. But William's early tantrums may also have been a sign that he was picking up on friction between his mother and father, and his mother's stressful transition from Lady Diana to the Princess of Wales. Perhaps William was unconsciously acting out his mother's feelings of frustration. It could be that as a terror toddler he was letting out the anger that the

later, quiet and thoughtful William prefered to repress.

Charles and Diana were doting parents and took part in school activities. To the external gaze, there were no obvious signs of the unhappy home life that later became so evident. These were often depicted as carefree years when William was able to grow, unburdened by his mother and father's troubles that were to shape his later life. But, under the surface, all was not well with the Waleses.

During the first term, he attended two mornings a week until half-term and then every weekday morning. In what was portrayed as a 'storybook' existence, William spent his first two terms in Cygnet Class before graduating to Big Swan Class. Names are given to classes, in this way, to foster group identification amongst the children. But would it ever be possible for William, dealing with such unique personal circumstances, to fit in? A common thread, which would run through William's later life, was already emerging in these early, awkward attempts to reconcile the 'ordinary' boy and the young Royal destined to be king.

As a Cygnet, William, a spontaneous young boy, enjoyed music and movement, painting and colouring and began to learn counting and letters. The school also placed emphasis on 'reporting news', encouraging the children to stand up and say what they had been doing outside school. William was able to tell his class about the Waleses' family holiday in Majorca with King Juan Carlos and Queen Sofia of Spain in August 1986. Even at a school where the children were from mainly privileged backgrounds, such things made William stand out as different. His parents' attempt to completely normalise William would always prove unsuccessful.

When William moved up into the Big Swan Class, he was taught blending sounds and reading words. He was very keen on reading and loved writing his name, gripping the pencil in his left hand. School trips with Mrs Mynors' to London Zoo and Hyde Park Police Station, central London, were highlights, even in the young life of a member of the Royal Family.

As William grew older these innocent and carefree pleasures would have to be left behind. The young Prince was to be introduced gradually to his formal responsibilities and predetermined roles. Diana was optimistic that the transition from childhood to adult royal status would be a gentle and, notably, natural one. For all of his parents'

attempts to encourage William to fit in with ordinary
people, the message was clear – royalty was in his blood. As
Diana pointed out, 'I always feel he will be all right because
he has been born to his royal role. He will get accustomed to
it gradually.'

Diana was immersed in William's school life. When she
was away from Wills, as the Waleses called him, the Princess
would chatter endlessly about him and any worries he had.
Like other mothers, she wanted the best for her son.

William first flew when he was not even two months old,
on 16 August 1982, when he travelled with his parents to
Aberdeen en route to Balmoral in the Scottish Highlands.
But perhaps a more significant milestone was his first flight
without Charles or Diana. In April 1985, he was a passenger,
with Nanny Barnes, on a scheduled British Airways service
to Aberdeen. It was something he would have to get used to.
In May 1985, William and Harry flew to Venice to join their
parents aboard the royal yacht, HMS *Britannia*, at the end
of the royal couple's official tour of Italy. William returned
from Sardinia four days later with Nanny Barnes on a
separate flight to his parents and brother. It had been
decided that he should travel alone in case an air accident
wiped out father, heir and spare. Already the reality of
being second in line to the throne was affecting William.

But being royal did have its advantages and, later that
month, an excited William accompanied the Prince of Wales
to watch the Red Devils Parachute Regiment free-fall at
Kensington Palace. A confident William loved the live
action-man display and, like many other boys his age, was
attracted to the world of military machismo. Later, in the
summer of 1986, the Parachute Regiment gave William and
Harry their own custom-made uniforms complete with child-
size berets. Also, even before starting nursery school,
William was taken by Charles and Diana on the Royals'
annual cruise of the Western Isles on *Britannia*.

Boyish misbehaviour continued to be a problem as
William showed little sign of calming down. His mischievous
nature was on display at the July 1986 wedding in
Westminster Abbey of his uncle, the Duke of York, to Sarah
Ferguson. William looked angelic in a white sailor's suit,
complete with straw boater. But his behaviour was far from
heavenly. While the other young pageboys and bridesmaids
sat still and behaved impeccably, probably overwhelmed by

Boyish misbehaviour continued to be a problem as William showed little sign of calming down.

the occasion, William fidgeted and stuck his tongue out at the little girls. He became absorbed with the elastic on his hat, snapping it and flicking it at young Alice Ferguson, the bride's half-sister. Whether or not this was attention-seeking behaviour by William, who may have been picking up on friction between his parents, the young Prince, clearly undaunted by his surroundings, was also showing early signs of becoming accustomed to his social status.

His parents hoped that a change of school would help improve William's behaviour and also decided the time was right to change nannies. The relatively liberal Barbara Barnes was replaced by Ruth Wallace, a brisk and businesslike woman who had worked with sick children before becoming nanny to the family of ex-King Constantine of Greece, these days exiled in London. At first, the change of nanny was confusing for William and Harry but the boys soon settled down and became fond of their new carer whom they called 'Roof'.

When Harry came onto the scene, William was jealous of the attention the younger and newest addition to the family received. The arrival of a brother may have intensified William's misbehaviour and attention-seeking. But, despite the possibility of sibling rivalry, the boys were to cement a long-term bond borne out of mutual experiences. Whatever their differences or disagreements, William and Harry had one important thing in common that few others could truly understand – they were both princes growing up in the glare of the public spotlight and they both knew the pressures – as well as the privileges – of being royal. Their father remarked, 'They are normal little boys who are unlucky enough to create an abnormal amount of attention.'

William was now poised for the next major step in his young life – infants' school. At the age of four-and-a-half, on 15 January 1987, he enrolled at Wetherby School, also in Notting Hill Gate and handy for Kensington Palace. He was to be a pupil there for more than three years, until 5 July 1990. Editors had again been informed and there was a press posse waiting to watch William arrive with his camera-conscious mother. His father was snowed in at Sandringham and was unable to be at the school.

Headmistress Miss Frederika Blair Turner took charge of the new pupil who, dressed in red-trimmed grey school uniform and cap, gave a cheeky wave to grateful

He was very keen on
reading and loved
writing his name,
gripping the pencil
in his left hand.

photographers. So far, William was playing to the cameras and there was no sign of the later shyness and reticence of his teenage years when he would hide his face.

William's teachers soon noted that he had a flair for English and spelling, and they remarked on his fine singing voice. He was encouraged to develop his strengths in and out of class. He sang in successive Christmas concerts, performing such Christmas favourites as 'Little Donkey', 'The Little Drummer Boy' – in which he also played a solo percussionist part – 'Silent Night' and 'In The Bleak Midwinter' with his classmates.

Drama was also encouraged and, in June 1990, he played the part of Sago the Skald in the school play, *The Saga of Erik Nobeard Or A Viking Nonetheless*. Diana went to the play but Charles was unable to as he had broken his arm playing polo and was in Cirencester Hospital nursing what turned out to be a troublesome and painful fracture.

A week earlier, on 21 June, William had celebrated his eighth birthday with friends at London Zoo, a treat organised by his mother. William liked the zoo and was showing an early interest in wild animals, setting him on the path to safaris in Africa.

Sports Day was held annually at Richmond Athletic Ground and both the Prince and Princess of Wales took part in parents' races. Like his mother, William was a powerful and stylish swimmer, and entered the school gala held each March at the Jubilee Sports Centre, west London. While in form four, he won the Grunfield Cup awarded to the boy with the best overall swimming style.

Holidays were plentiful for the young Prince and the Royal Family's connections gave the Waleses access to exclusive and luxurious places that few people could imagine visiting, even after a lifetime of hard work. Part of the 1986 and 1987 school summer holidays were spent with the Spanish Royals in their palace on Majorca. The Waleses also visited the Spanish sunshine island with Juan Carlos and his family in 1988 and 1990. At the end of May 1988, William and Harry, accompanied by Nanny Wallace and police bodyguard Dave 'Razor' Sharp, went to St Mary's in the Scilly Isles. The following year, William and his brother returned to the Scillies, this time visiting Tresco. Early in January 1989, William, Harry and Diana went on holiday to Necker in the Virgin Islands. The Caribbean island, owned

by Virgin tycoon Richard Branson, had been made available by him to Diana and her family as a secluded and private retreat and they were there again in April 1990. Also, in the summer of 1989, William stayed with a school friend in Portugal. Trusty royal protection officer Dave Sharp, a likeable and fatherly character, went with him.

If these frequent jaunts to exclusive locations make William and Harry look somewhat spoilt, it is well to remember that other holiday destinations, open to ordinary people, are out of bounds to the Princes. Spontaneity is a luxury the Princes do not enjoy when travelling.

'He was just so excited by it all. He was so organised that he chose his own shorts and shirt. It's best to let him do that if you want him to smile at the cameras!'

Princess of Wales, September 1985

4

HOME AND AWAY

Going to boarding school was a big step for the eight-year-old William, and seeing him go was a wrench for Diana, who knew she would miss her first-born. But boarding was a tradition within the Royal Family and no alternative was seriously considered.

Ludgrove School at Wokingham in Berkshire had been carefully chosen. Charles and Diana were impressed by its facilities and academic record and also by the pastoral care offered to pupils. Boarding school had been a trial for Charles and he was anxious that William should not suffer in the same way.

Accompanied by his parents, William arrived at the prep school on 10 September 1990, at 10.30 a.m., and was met by headmasters Nichol Marston and Gerald Barber with his wife, Jane. It was an ordeal but the new pupil remained composed, while his mother dissolved in tears. At first William was homesick but, after a while, he settled in. He treasured letters written to him by Diana who addressed him as 'My Darling Wombat'. So precious was his mother's correspondence that William locked the letters in his school tuck-box.

Charles Spencer, by now the ninth Earl Spencer, described his nephew at this time as 'a very self-possessed, intelligent and mature boy, and quite shy. He is quite formal and stiff, sounding older than his years when he answers the phone.' The over-exuberance of his earlier years had disappeared and William had become a cautious, somewhat introverted boy. His parents' marriage problems, publicly denied and hidden from outsiders, seemed to have taken their toll on a once spontaneous youngster.

William spent the next five years at Ludgrove until 5 July 1995. Other pupils noted that, at times, he seemed weighed down by worry, walking alone in the secluded school grounds with his shoulders hunched. However, he applied himself to academic work and during this time developed his flair for English, winning the Junior Essay Prize in the summer term of 1992. He also began to show an interest in geography, which was to endure throughout his academic career, and was a full school monitor in his final year. Signs of his developing caring nature and social conscience were evident in May 1994, and the following year, when he went on sponsored walks for the Wokingham and District Association for the Elderly.

The young Prince's sporting ability and competitive edge came to the fore at Ludgrove where he was a rugby and hockey team captain, a useful footballer, basketball player and represented the school at cross-country running and swimming. In July 1994, William won the Cliddesden Salver for clay pigeon shooting, continuing a long royal tradition in the sport. Both Charles and Diana encouraged William to take part in sport. His boyish body was starting to develop into a strong, sporty physique and he enjoyed keeping fit. But there was probably more to taking part in sport than simply playing the game. Sporting prowess also gained William the respect he desired from his peers without reference to his royal status. Team sports further enabled him to feel accepted by the other boys as a valuable member of a unit, irrespective of who he was. At a difficult time, physical exercise, like academic endeavour, may have been a source of solace for William as well as a distraction from worldly woes.

William was no longer the cheeky, outgoing youngster, but if his childhood tantrums had been a means of seeking attention, he was now gaining the recognition he seemed to crave as a top sportsman and gifted student.

Charles and Diana, despite their own personal differences, continued to share in William's school life and, in June 1995, the Prince of Wales took part with William in the father-and-son clay pigeon shooting competition. William was fast becoming a crack shot but, despite her pride in his achievements, Diana did not favour shooting and her royal son's inevitable participation in blood sports. Tennis was more her thing and, in July that year, the Princess teamed up with William to play in the mother-and-son tennis tournament. Despite some teenage self-consciousness at being seen with his parents by school friends, added to by a heightened sense of embarrassment at Charles and Diana's public notoriety, these were special occasions for William. However, when together, Charles and Diana were often at war and their sensitive, elder son had to make do with quality time with each of them separately rather than as a family.

William's school acting career blossomed with appearances in the 1990, 1993 and 1994 Christmas plays. In March 1993, the boy destined to be king played Emperor Napoleon in *The Sword of General Frapp* by John Harris.

Wearing Napoleonic costume, assuming the dramatic air of nineteenth-century French nobility, William cut a fine figure as he walked on stage. Of course, even among the pupils, parents and staff of Ludgrove, he was no ordinary boy and his entrance caused a stir. But William, who was secretary of the school dramatic society, simply wanted to be treated like anyone else.

While a pupil at Ludgrove, William began to make an appearance on the public stage as a member of the Royal Family. But his role was to be a supporting one and was undertaken reluctantly. With Prince Harry, he accompanied his mother to St Paul's Cathedral, London, in October 1990, for a service to commemorate the fiftieth anniversary of the Blitz, the bombing of Britain during the early years of World War II. In December that year he went with the Princess to a Christmas music concert by the London Symphony Chorus at the Barbican. Signing the visitors' book – his first public signature – William confirmed to the watching world that he was left-handed.

His first official public engagement was on 1 March 1991, when he accompanied his mother and father to Wales on St David's Day. He attended a service at Llandaff Cathedral, Cardiff, and then went with Diana to a ceremony in St David's Hall in the Welsh capital, while Charles visited RAF Brawdy. Even alongside his world-famous and photogenic mother, William was the centre of attention. Diana, full of pride, tried to help her son take his first steps as a public Royal, while a supportive Charles coached him on what to do and what was expected of him. William seemed shy and a little overwhelmed by the adulation of the crowds, as he often would be in his later life. But he behaved with impeccable good manners, delighting onlookers. His popularity was already clear as he set out on a long journey towards his destiny of kingship.

In April 1991, William went on a skiing holiday in the Austrian resort of Lech with his mother and brother, accompanied by Viscount Linley and Catherine Soames. In May, he went with Harry, Charles and Diana to Tresco in the Scilly Islands.

Back at school, on 3 June, William was at the centre of a major drama. He was admitted to the Royal Berkshire Hospital in Reading with a depressed fracture of the forehead after an accident on the school putting green.

William had been playing with a friend when he was hit on the side of the head with a golf club. Despite the severity of the blow, the young Prince was not knocked out. 'Prince William was very brave and did not cry,' nurses said. His parents were immediately alerted after the accident and rushed to his side. Accompanied by a worried Princess of Wales, William was transferred by ambulance to London's Great Ormond Street Hospital for Sick Children. The Prince of Wales followed behind in his car.

The Queen's Physician and Head of the Medical Household, Anthony Dawson, was consulted and that evening William underwent a seventy-minute operation and needed twenty-four stitches. He was visited the following morning by Harry and, later in the day, by his father. William was accommodated in a private wing of the hospital for security reasons and to minimise disruption to other patients. The Princess remained at William's bedside until, on 6 June, he left the hospital to go home to Kensington Palace. After more than two weeks recuperation, William returned to Ludgrove, still accompanied by his attentive mother who drove him back to school for the last fortnight of term.

The school summer holiday saw treats for William who in July went with Diana, a great tennis fan, to Ladies' Finals Day at Wimbledon. A family holiday, accompanied by ex-King Constantine and Queen Anne-Marie of Greece and their children, followed in August. The royal party cruised the Mediterranean aboard the MV *Alexander*, the luxury yacht belonging to the Prince of Wales's wealthy friend John Latsis, calling at Naples, Sardinia and Menorca.

Being royal had its obvious benefits and the holidays, packed with water sports, were a welcome distraction. But William resented being in the public eye, especially when his mother and father's failing marriage was increasingly becoming a matter of public knowledge and front-page news. As far as possible, he was shielded from the newspaper headlines. Tabloid papers were kept out of his sight and he rarely watched TV news or listened to radio reports.

Before the close of 1991, William went with Charles, Diana and Harry on an official visit to Canada. But as well as official duties, Diana was determined that William and Harry should have fun and experience the same things as other youngsters. She took William and Harry on trips to

Being royal had its
obvious benefits and the
holidays, packed with
water sports, were a
welcome distraction.

Cardiff Arms Park to see Wales play France at rugby, one of his favourite sports, and to the London film premiere of *Hook*, starring Dustin Hoffman and Robin Williams. They also went to the Dinosaur Exhibition at London's Natural History Museum and on a return trip – they had been the previous Easter – to Thorpe Park, Surrey, for daredevil water rides. William, who loved the exhilaration of speed, adored the Log Flume and Rapids Ride. Later, William and Harry were to experience riding real rapids when they went white-water rafting on holiday in Colorado, USA. Back home, Alton Towers, an adventure park in Staffordshire, was also a popular venue for Diana and her boys.

The next family holiday – skiing in Lech in March 1992 – was cut short by the death of William's maternal grandfather, Earl Spencer. A devastated Diana returned home with the Prince of Wales. Even in mourning, Charles and Diana were unreconciled. The Princess had wanted to return to Britain alone but was persuaded that, for the sake of outward appearances at least, she should be accompanied by her husband, although she felt little comfort from him.

In August that year the Waleses took another cruise on the *Alexander*, this time around the Greek islands and Cyprus. It was to be their last family holiday. It seemed William's parents could no longer bear to be together, even for the sake of their sons.

If William arrived at Ludgrove with the weight of his parents' troubled marriage on his young shoulders, he would leave having suffered as a casualty of their separation.

Charles and Diana's life together was an emotional roller-coaster ride, with more downs than ups. Theirs had been the wedding of the century and the birth of two sons seemed the perfect endorsement of a happy union. But almost from the start, Diana showed signs of stress and felt trapped inside the Royal Family. Looking thin and strained after the birth of William, she was said to be suffering from post-natal depression. Following the birth of Harry, rows became more frequent, and Charles and Diana started to lead increasingly separate lives. By 1987, signs of a rift were prompting media speculation. Diana was suspicious of her husband's relationship with his old flame, Camilla Parker Bowles, and began to spend time with her Old Etonian friend, car salesman James Gilbey. In March 1991, the Princess's close friendship with cavalry officer Captain

James Hewitt became public knowledge.

The royal marriage crisis came to a head in 1992 when a book by former royal journalist Andrew Morton blew the lid off the sham their marriage had become. Diana had secretly collaborated with the author whose book claimed she was trapped inside a loveless marriage. It revealed she was suffering the eating disorder bulimia nervosa and had, on a number of occasions, inflicted violent self-harm while threatening to kill herself. Shortly after, details were published of an intimate telephone conversation between Diana and James Gilbey, dubbed 'Dianagate', in which Gilbey affectionately called the Princess 'Squidgy' and she revealed her bitterness towards the Royal Family. A formal separation was now inevitable.

Charles and Diana's decision to part was announced in the House of Commons by Prime Minister John Major on 9 December 1992. William had already been informed privately by the Princess who had gone to see him at Ludgrove a few days earlier. Mr Major, speaking to a hushed Commons, insisted there would be no constitutional implications arising from the royal separation, and no divorce. He said nothing of the emotional impact on William and his brother Harry.

William, the elder boy, was particularly sensitive to his parents' marriage problems. Diana's friends thought she talked to her elder son as if the youngster was an adult. She treated him as a confidant, infuriating Charles who thought she should not involve William in their marital politics. When William was at home, there was a constant atmosphere between Charles and Diana. The Princess could not hide her unhappiness and it seemed she had not learnt from her own troubled childhood how emotionally damaging this could be for William. Diana was damaged by a broken home – and history was repeating itself.

At Highgrove, the Prince of Wales's Gloucestershire mansion, Charles and Diana might as well have been living in separate houses. The family rarely ate together, for instance, with Charles left alone at the dining table while William and Harry had a tray-meal, watching television with the Princess in her room.

There was a dark side to Diana in contrast to the glamorous, caring individual portrayed in public. At home she would snap at Charles and the servants, and could manipulate

William and his brother to spite their father. William often found his mother crying and must have been confused by the grown-ups' squabbles. He desperately wanted his parents to love each other and could not understand why they rowed. Charles and Diana both loved their children, but the Prince and Princess did not love each other.

William showed signs of feeling humiliated by the public airing of his parents' problems. Already shy of photographers, he appeared embarrassed, hanging his head as if he felt some kind of shame. He did not want to be pitied, he just wanted to be an ordinary boy.

After the marriage break up, William's spare time outside school was to be divided between Diana at Kensington Palace and Charles at Highgrove. There would be trips abroad with either the Prince or the Princess, but the Waleses would never be seen again as a family unit, except for high-profile official occasions.

For years, William and Harry had been the only thing keeping Charles and Diana together; now it seemed the boys were the only thing between their parents and divorce.

Something for William to look forward to during this difficult time was a New Year holiday in Nevis in the Caribbean with Diana and Harry, which the Princess hoped would soften the blow of her separation from Charles. This was followed by a skiing holiday for mother and sons in Lech at the end of March. Charles took William and Harry on a Greek islands cruise aboard MV *Alexander* in August.

The trips away were wonderful but there can be little doubt that William and Harry felt as if they were caught in a tug-of-love between their mother and father. William seemed to react by assuming the role of protective big brother to Harry. For emotional as well as institutional reasons, bearing in mind his parents' difficulties and his closeness to the throne, William had to grow up quickly.

Following the formal separation, Charles sought help to bring up William and Harry, and employed thirty-year-old Tiggy Legge-Bourke as a nanny, although she was to become more like a surrogate mother. Diana already felt displaced in her marriage by Camilla. Now there was also a rival for her boys' affection.

Skiing figured large in William's life and, after a shaky start, he was by now confident on the mountain slopes. His parents' separation meant William, with Harry, had two

family skiing holidays a year in 1994 and 1995: one each year with Charles in the Prince of Wales's favourite Swiss resort of Klosters, accompanied by the Palmer-Tomkinson family; and one each year with Diana in Lech. In fact, after Lech in 1994, William went with friends on a third skiing trip, also in Austria, to Obergurgl.

Possessive of her sons, the Princess had already, in March 1994, taken them on a private visit to Paris. The short break was followed in the summer by a Mediterranean cruise with their father aboard the *Alexander* after William had been on holiday to Corfu, the birthplace of his paternal grandfather, the Duke of Edinburgh, with his school friend Ned Barrie. Watched over by policeman Trevor Bettles, William spent the last day in Athens, on a guided tour, while waiting for his flight home.

Holidays were not simply about leisure but also represented the continuing struggle between Charles and Diana to retain the full affection and loyalty of their boys. Each parent desired time alone with their children which meant a doubling of the number of holidays abroad. But for the boys these trips must have raised ambivalent emotions. The absence of either parent must have lent a poignant air to any more joyful experiences. Whether or not it was ever said, William and Harry must have felt they were being manipulated by their parents, who wished not just to protect their children's feelings, but also to safeguard their own positions in the boys' lives.

Media representations of the various holidays may also have been confusing for the young boys. Diana was seen as the down-to-earth, populist and caring mother who took her boys on fun-filled trips. Holidays with Charles were portrayed as formal, stuffy and elitist. 'Touchy-feely' Diana was pictured hugging her boys while a more reserved Charles rarely showed such public demonstrations of his undoubted affection. In truth, Charles was equally demonstrative but mainly in private, away from the cameras.

June 1994 saw the TV screening of an interview with the Prince of Wales by his latest biographer, Jonathan Dimbleby. During the programme, Charles admitted adultery after the irreconcilable breakdown of his marriage. It was the first public confirmation of his continuing relationship with Mrs Camilla Parker Bowles, whose marriage to Brigadier Andrew Parker Bowles would be

dissolved the following March. More bad news for William and more public humiliation for his family.

After the separation, the Waleses' first official 'family' outing, with Charles and Diana appearing together with their children for the sake of public duty, came on 7 May 1995. William, with Diana and Harry, joined Charles in the Blue Drawing Room at Buckingham Palace prior to travelling to London's Hyde Park by coach to attend a heads of state and government ceremony, commemorating the fiftieth anniversary of victory in Europe over Nazi Germany. Despite their outward solidarity, there was little love shown between William's warring parents. Such occasions were clearly an ordeal for Charles and Diana, and were understandably a strain for William and Harry.

However, the year improved for William who in May attended the FA Cup Final between Everton and Manchester United at Wembley with Charles and Harry. An all-round sportsman, except for a curious lack of interest in cricket, William loved the atmosphere of a big sporting final. He had no particular allegiance to either team – he supports Aston Villa, although why William chose the Midlands club is unclear.

In June, good news came when the royal press office at St James's Palace announced that William had passed the Common Entrance exam to Eton College. Diana had been instrumental in choosing Eton for William, who would follow in the footsteps of her Old Etonian father, Earl Spencer, and brother Charles Spencer. Situated across the River Thames from Windsor Castle, the elite Berkshire public school was also convenient for the Royal Family.

But first there were fun holidays in Colorado with Diana, and aboard the luxury *Alexander* with Charles, cruising around the Greek islands.

A further milestone in William's royal career was recorded on 19 August 1995, when he had his first mention in the Court Circular, the report of the Royals' daily public engagements issued by Buckingham Palace and published in up-market newspapers. With his mother, father and brother, he had joined the Queen and other members of the Royal Family in The Mall, central London, to mark the fiftieth anniversary of VJ Day – victory in Japan and the end of the Second World War. William and Harry spent that night aboard HMS *Britannia* and watched a military flypast and impressive fireworks display.

Diana was determined
that William and Harry
should have fun and
experience the same
things as other youngsters.

5

YOUNG ETONIAN – TEENAGER

Dressed in a smart tweed jacket, grey trousers, collar and tie, a fresh-faced William arrived at Eton College on 6 September 1995, for the start of term – and his senior school career.

The thirteen-year-old had already attended a new boys' lunch, accompanied by his mother, at Manor House four days earlier. This was to be his home-from-home for the next five years and, after meeting his fellow new boys and their parents, William had been shown around the house. His room was the same as other boys' and would soon be personalised by the young Prince with his belongings.

The only difference for William was that a police protection officer had a room nearby. The Prince was guarded around-the-clock by plain-clothed, armed officers who were never far away. When William walked through Eton or to Windsor for tea or to a shop, for instance, he was followed at a discreet distance by two officers in business suits, with guns holstered under their jackets. In an often claustrophobic existence, William is always being watched, if not by the media, by his bodyguards. For all the things royal life has given him, it has taken away the true independence of a young man growing up.

Diana was in the driving seat when the estranged Waleses arrived by car with William for the start of term. They were met by William's housemaster, Dr Andrew Gailey, a relatively young history teacher from Northern Ireland, who was to guide the pupil Prince through his time at Eton.

Charles, Diana, William and Harry posed with Dr Gailey at the gate of Manor House for the invited mass media, there to capture the moment for a curious public. A somewhat shy but smiling William had to be encouraged to lift his head for the photographers and cameramen who called out from a specially erected riser across the road.

The royal party proceeded to the Upper School where, in one of Eton's ancient buildings, William enrolled by signing the historic school register. Watched by headmaster John Lewis, a New Zealander, and assisted by Charles and Diana, William signed the book.

Eton is a royal foundation, established more than five centuries ago in 1440 by King Henry VI, himself only eighteen at the time. The King's College of Our Lady of Eton beside Windsor, as it was originally called, was

intended to provide scholars for another royal foundation, King's College, Cambridge, and so ensure a ready supply of learned men to administer royal government.

Today, it remains an all-boys' school, now for 1,280 pupils, taught by 150 full-time masters, and is undeniably posh, with a long history of turning out upper-crust Englishmen to run the country and the military. Indeed, over the years, the exclusive school has provided twenty prime ministers, including Walpole, Pitt the Elder, William Gladstone and Harold Macmillan, as well as writers like Shelley and George Orwell. Other famous Old Etonians include economist Maynard Keynes, Captain Oates, of Scott's ill-fated expedition to the South Pole, and numerous soldiers of whom the latest Victoria Cross holder was Colonel H. Jones who died a hero in the 1982 Falklands War with Argentina. In the eighteenth century, two Old Etonians, Thomas Lynch and Thomas Nelson, signed the American Declaration of Independence.

These days money talks at the school and alongside the sons of the gentry and the aristocracy are the offspring of millionaire rock stars and business magnates.

With all its historic past, Eton's traditions provide the context for a thoroughly modern education, combining high academic expectations with wide-ranging opportunities in sport, drama, music and the arts. Facilities include three theatres, two concert halls and two major libraries and, although some buildings are old, they are equipped with the very latest technology.

The day after his arrival, William stepped out to his first lesson, dressed in Eton's distinctive uniform, looking dashing in black tailcoat, waistcoat, pinstriped trousers and a stiff white collar. The media were again present to record the event. They had been invited as part of a deal with the royal press office at St James's Palace, backed by the watchdog Press Complaints Commission, whereby journalists would be given stories and pictures at significant junctures in William's life in return for allowing him privacy while in full-time education. Editors agreed not to dispatch their staff to pester William and not to buy freelance pictures of him, thus stopping the paparazzi.

The boys at Eton are divided up into twenty-four houses named after the resident housemaster who is primarily responsible for the fifty boys in his charge. In

'I enjoy dancing
but don't go
clubbing that often.'

William's case, Dr Gailey, a graduate of St Andrews and
Cambridge Universities and author of occasional books on
Anglo-Irish relations in the nineteenth and twentieth
centuries, acted as guardian. Married with one daughter,
Dr Gailey was supported in dealing with pupils' domestic
matters by matron Elizabeth Heathcote who was probably
the most important woman in William's life at Eton.

The dame, as matrons are called at Eton, helped
William through the emotional strains of term-time,
especially when news from home was worrying. Miss
Heathcote, who was in her fifties, was herself the daughter
of an Old Etonian and had worked at the school for nearly
thirty years. With Dr Gailey, she was to prove a tower of
strength for William when his life was turned upside down.

Manor House occupies one of the oldest sites in Eton
and is where the Duke of Wellington boarded. His portrait
dominates the main hall and reminded William of the
history and tradition of his new school, not that he was a
stranger to such things. If the Iron Duke really did assert
that the Battle of Waterloo was 'won on the playing fields
of Eton', it was probably the gardens to the rear of Manor
House to which he was referring. The house was the centre
of William's life at Eton. He ate, studied and slept there,
and much of his sport was played in the Manor House
colours of fawn and blue.

At the outset, William and the nine other new boys
in his house had to learn Eton-speak, a strange new
language. Teachers were 'beaks', lessons 'schools' and
homework 'EWs' or 'extra work'. The school term was
called a 'half' despite there being three a year, a practice
dating from the sixteenth century when there were only
two terms each year.

There is a tradition at Eton of boys etching their names
on walls and furniture, the sort of graffiti that would be an
offence in a state school. Famous names in the cloisters
include Shelley, Gladstone and Walpole. However, only
pupils whose fathers were at Eton may join in the tradition,
and this excluded Prince William, whose father went to
Gordonstoun in Scotland.

Initially William studied English, Latin, French,
geography, history, divinity, mathematics, chemistry,
biology and physics, along with courses in art, music
and design, as well as PE or gym. Despite his distressing

family problems, he performed extremely well, scoring high grades in his national GCSE exams. He took Latin and French GCSEs in 1997 and achieved the highest 'A-star' grades. The following year William scored 'A-star' in biology, 'A's in English, English literature, geography, history and Spanish and 'B's in maths and additional French.

William's ten GCSEs delighted his family and marked him out to be one of the most academic members of the Windsor dynasty, destined for greater achievements in the sixth form and at university. It seems likely that William felt some sort of sanctuary at Eton, sheltering from his parents' nagging marital disagreements and out of the public spotlight. While at Eton he could at least seek solace in his schoolwork.

But William's examination success was achieved despite personal heartache. In November 1995, his mother told a TV audience of twenty-three million people of her infidelity with James Hewitt, the polo-playing cavalryman who had helped William improve his horsemanship. In her blockbuster interview for the BBC's *Panorama*, Diana blamed Camilla Parker Bowles for the breakdown of her marriage and questioned whether the Prince of Wales was suited to be king.

Airing all this 'dirty washing' in public was bad enough, but now William's mother was putting him forward in competition with his father as the next king. What was William to think? He did not want to be involved in this undignified and humiliating fight, which Diana was fast turning into a direct challenge to the authority of the monarchy and Charles's right to the throne. He did not want to usurp his father. Apart from the personal loyalty he felt towards the Prince of Wales, William knew the line of succession in an hereditary monarchy should not be tampered with.

After the intervention of the Queen who was determined to end the damaging war of the Waleses, it was announced that William's parents would divorce. Charles and Diana's fifteen-year marriage was officially ended on 28 August 1996. William had grown up with his parents' marital problems but still the final dissolution of their union was traumatic and played on his mind. However, he hoped the future would be brighter and that his mother

and father would now be happier. He wished his parents
could at least be friends, which, to some extent, would help
heal the wounds inflicted on the family by Charles and
Diana's turmoil.

One of the last times the Waleses were together was on
9 March 1997, when William was confirmed at St George's
Chapel, Windsor, by the Bishop of London, Richard
Chartres. Diana was reunited with her ex-husband and
other senior Royals at the service. Now they were no longer
husband and wife, Charles and Diana did seem to be more
civil to each other.

But in early June, William took the brave decision to
ask both his mother and father to stay away from Eton
parents' day. He felt the attention of the media would
spoil the occasion for other pupils and their parents.
Instead he invited his former nanny Tiggy Legge-Bourke
and his good friend William van Cutsem. Without his
divorced parents present, William seemed at greater ease,
smiling and chatting.

Later that month, at Christie's in New York, Diana
realised a charity fundraising idea devised by William.
Her son had suggested that she should auction some of
her dresses to help good causes. The resulting fundraiser
was the gowns sale of the century, making more than £2
million, for which Diana gave William full credit.

A Mediterranean holiday followed in July for Diana and
her sons at the St Tropez villa of Harrods' owner Mohamed
Al Fayed in the south of France. It was to be their last
together. Diana returned to the Mediterranean in August
to spend time with her new boyfriend, Mr Al Fayed's film
producer son, Dodi. After the trauma of her divorce, she
at last seemed happy. No one could have known that the
Princess, who was only thirty-six-years-old, had less than a
month to live.

Few people will ever forget the shock they felt when the
news of Diana's death was broadcast to the world. She died
on 31 August 1997, from fatal injuries sustained in a high-
speed car crash in a dingy Paris underpass. Dodi Al Fayed
also died, along with the chauffeur of their car.

William and his brother were with the Royal Family at
Balmoral in Scotland when their father broke the awful
news. In the immediate aftermath of the death, which
prompted an unprecedented outpouring of national grief,

'I don't like the attention. I feel
uncomfortable with it, but I have
particularly appreciated being left
alone at Eton, which has allowed me
to concentrate on my school work
and enjoy being with my friends
without being followed by cameras.'

William remained at Balmoral, comforted by his grandmother the Queen and counselled by his cousin Peter Phillips, son of the Princess Royal. Momentous personal grief filled William's heart but he conducted himself with the decorum expected of the high-profile public figure he had become.

In one of the most memorable scenes of any lifetime, William, with Harry, the Prince of Wales, Earl Spencer and the Duke of Edinburgh, walked solemnly behind Diana's coffin in a funeral cortège through the streets of central London. William, like his brother, showed great composure and his stature grew in the minds of the millions weeping for his mother – and for Diana's brave boys.

More drama was to come as the late Princess's brother Charles, Earl Spencer, delivered a forthright and powerful funeral oration that risked creating a rift between the Spencers, Diana's 'blood family', and the House of Windsor. From the pulpit of Westminster Abbey, he said in Diana's memory, 'On behalf of your [Diana's] mother and sisters I pledge that we, your blood family, will do all we can to continue the imaginative and loving way in which you were steering these two exceptional young men [William and Harry] so their souls are not simply immersed by duty and tradition but can sing openly as planned.'

Earl Spencer may have been promising more than he could hope to deliver and he was certainly speaking from the heart. But how did this apparent attack on the Prince of Wales and the Royal Family, who, he seemed to be implying, would stifle the Princes with their rigid and old-fashioned ways, effect William and Harry? They must have felt torn between their mother's family and their father, grieving at their side. Once the victims of a tug-of-love between parents, William and Harry were now the victims of a public tug-of-war.

The whole world seemed to be mourning his mother's death while William felt his own personal loss. Did he now reflect on what his mother had meant to those people who left a sea of flowers outside Kensington Palace? At a time of such great trauma, it may have been too difficult to contemplate how ordinary people identified with Diana, sometimes glamorous and compassionate, other times sad and lonely. But the empathy shown by millions, for

whatever reasons, may have helped William. He knew he was not alone in his sorrow.

The Prince of Wales later spoke of his admiration for William and Harry's courage on the day of their mother's funeral. As he walked with the two young Princes behind his ex-wife's coffin, Charles was his boys' support. It was a scene that was to be repeated in April 2002 when the principal male Royals walked in the Queen Mother's funeral cortège. But this time it was William who lent support to his devastated father, whose face was etched with grief at the loss of his beloved grandmother. William's experience of loss as a teenager meant the empathy he showed his father was deeper than might ordinarily be expected of someone his age.

The death of Diana is understandably a sensitive and painful subject for William and, to date, he has chosen not to talk about it in public. However, on his first birthday without his mother, William gave an exclusive interview for the Press Association, the UK news agency.

Cautiously answering written questions – a practice followed by other Royals, including his mother when interviewed in Angola during her world campaign against the use of landmines – William showed himself to be impressively diplomatic for such a young man. He declined to name his favourite pop bands for fear of upsetting the ones he left out. Similarly, he would not express a preference for university. Perhaps such guarded answers betrayed the excessive restrictions and control over his young life.

However, the sixteen-year-old Prince did give some insight into his tastes and interests. He said reading was a favourite pastime, particularly action-adventure fiction and non-fiction. He also liked action films and computer games. An ambition, which he was soon to realise, was to go on safari in Africa to see big game in the wild. Because of commitments at Eton, he had missed out in 1997 when Harry went on safari in Botswana while their father was visiting southern Africa.

Like his father, William enjoyed writing letters and also kept in touch with family and friends by telephone. At Highgrove, he had a pet female black Labrador, called Widgeon, and he shared the Royal Family's love of horses but did not have his own.

William revealed that he liked fast food, enjoyed shopping for his own clothes and liked modern styles. Despite the restrictions placed on him by his royal position, William does have much greater freedom as a modern Prince than his father had at his age. At Eton, in particular, he was left alone by the media and was able to exercise this relative freedom to do some of the ordinary things others take for granted. Visiting the local clothes shops was far more enjoyable for William than having a retailer bring in samples to Kensington Palace or Highgrove. Choosing his own clothes was an important way for the Prince to express his individuality, especially in the world of the Royals where formality and protocol usually dictate dress codes.

At that time William was rivalling Hollywood movie star Leonardo DiCaprio as the top teen pin-up, and in the interview he tried to explain how he dealt with the attention of girl fans.

William's final two years at Eton were a preparation for university. He chose to study for A-level exams in history of art, geography and biology. By now Harry had enrolled at Eton and was a boarder with William in Manor House. The two boys were to be a support for each other in the difficult years after the loss of their mother. William helped Harry feel at home at Eton. They saw each other at meal times and were able spend free time together until Harry built up his own circle of friends.

Lessons were from 9 a.m. until 11.20 a.m. when there was a twenty-five-minute break after which classes resumed until 1.15 p.m. After lunch there were two further hours of lessons. William had to be in his room by 11 p.m.

In addition to his academic studies, William took optional sixth-form courses in motorcycle maintenance and cookery. His A-level coursework involved visits to London art galleries, including the Tate, the Victoria and Albert Museum, the Royal Academy and the National Gallery, and geography field trips to Thame in Oxfordshire, London Docklands, Dartmoor and north-east England, as well as attending lectures at the Royal Society.

While in the first year of the sixth form at Eton, William joined the Combined Cadet Corps, which gives public school boys basic military training and the chance to experience some aspects of a soldier's life. To the great

pleasure of the Prince of Wales, William excelled. Marching in time with royal tradition, he was a member of the winning drill syndicate at the annual passing out parade in December 1998, attended by his proud father. Charles was also at the Eton Tattoo in June 1999 to witness William winning the Sword of Honour as top first-year cadet. William took part in numerous cadet corps exercises and during the 1999 summer camp he swam in the winning triathlon team at Fishguard in Wales. The teenage Prince's interest in the school corps heightened speculation that one day he could follow his royal predecessors and serve in the armed forces, possibly with the Welsh Guards.

Sport continued to play a major part in William's life outside the classroom. He was a keen rugby player, reaching the second XV as a flanker, until a broken finger stopped him playing. The injury occurred during the Senior House Sevens competition before Christmas 1998 but at first William did not realise its severity. An X-ray early in the New Year confirmed the finger was broken and when, in April, the injury was still troublesome, it was decided that the Prince needed surgery. An operation was carried out, under general anaesthetic, in the Pulvertaft Hand Centre at Derbyshire Royal Infirmary to stabilise the fractured bone with pins and wires. Untreated, the injury could have caused arthritis in the Prince's hand later in life.

On 15 April, William was seen in London with his hand in a sling when he became godfather to Prince Konstantine Alexios of Greece, the baby son of Greek Crown Prince and Crown Princess Pavlos. A resigned Prince of Wales once remarked that such injuries seemed to be a regular occurrence for both his sports-mad boys. In fact, William and Harry's father has himself picked up more than his fair share of sports injuries during his polo career.

No longer able to play school rugby, William took to an historic, and to an outsider, puzzling sport – said to have inspired Harry Potter's 'Quidditch' – the Eton Wall Game. The object of the game is to get a ball slightly smaller than a football to one or other end of the 118-yard brick wall that separates the playing fields of Eton from Slough Road. Although players wear protective gloves, it is doubtful whether William's damaged hand was safe from harm in a game described as 'open warfare'.

William also became a passionate devotee of the Eton
Field Game, which is a mixture of rugby and football,
using smaller, hockey-sized goals. But prime among his
many sporting interests were swimming and especially
water polo. He represented Eton in both from the outset,
eventually gaining double school colours. He was under-
sixteen 50m freestyle champion in 1997, and in March
1998 won both the senior 50m and 100m freestyle
competitions. In March 1999, he was runner-up in the
senior diving competition. Water polo took priority over
other sports in the sixth form and William was a regular
member of Eton's successful teams, playing up front.

He played all major sports for his house, except that
most English of games, cricket. As a first-year pupil, he
tried rowing on the River Thames but did not take to
being, in Eton-speak, a 'Wet Bob'. As house captain of
games, he led the football team to the semi-finals of the
House Ties, the main school competition. He played in
central defence and followed the Etonian custom of
wearing odd socks for the game. Other sporting interests
included hockey, cross-country running and latterly polo,
playing for the Eton team, although handicapped by his
hand injury. For safety reasons polo cannot be played left-
handed, so southpaw William has to play right-handed.

Polo, a passion of his father and brother, has since
assumed greater importance in William's sporting life and
he now likes to play as often as possible. Very much the
reserve of the rich, polo also presents a glamorous social
scene, frequented by the wealthy, the beautiful and those
with the money to make themselves attractive. Not only
William's royal status and good looks but also his ability
and skilful horsemanship make him a focus of attention
for devotees of the sport as well as socialites, young
unmarried women included. In the summer of 1999,
William and Harry played in the same team as the Prince
of Wales for the first time.

Another country pursuit favoured by the Royals is
marksmanship and during school holidays the Prince went
on private shoots at Windsor, Balmoral, Sandringham,
Douglas, Abbeystead, Mossdale and Gunnerside.

William's interest in drama continued, but he no longer
chose to take centre stage. He went to plays at the Royal
Shakespeare Company in Stratford and at the Theatre

'I like to keep my
private life private.'

Royal, Windsor, as well as school productions. He took a small part, an Attendant Lord, in a production of *The Tempest* that was performed at Eton in February 1998 with his grandparents, the Queen and the Duke of Edinburgh, in the audience. On a different cultural tack, in March 1999 he went with other Etonians to see the London stage version of the hit disco movie *Saturday Night Fever*.

William has inherited a talent for painting from the Prince of Wales and finds the pastime both enjoyable and relaxing. Diana had loved to collect William's paintings and he delighted in giving her his best work, which became some of the Princess's most treasured possessions.

In his final year at Eton, William held a number of positions of responsibility within the school. These included secretary of the Agricultural Society, reflecting his keen interest in the countryside, joint 'keeper' or captain of swimming and house captain of games. Later, in April 2000, he was elevated to house captain.

William was also elected to the Eton Society or 'Pop'. Founded in 1811 as a debating society, meeting in Mrs Hatton's lollipop shop which then stood on a site adjacent to Manor House, it has since become the main prefectorial body for the school. William was one of twenty-one prefects, distinguishable by their dress of 'sponge-bag' trousers – similar to chinos – stiff wing collar and white bow tie, braid-edged black tailcoat and a colourful waistcoat of their choosing. Among William's fancy 'Pop' waistcoats were Union Jack and large polka-dot designs. He also had a waistcoat made in the claret and blue colours of his favourite football team, Aston Villa, and in the fawn and blue of Manor House.

Life outside school changed dramatically during William's sixth-form years. The death of Diana meant he now spent more time with his father. In July 1998, before returning to Eton for the start of the lower sixth, William and Harry organised an early, surprise fiftieth birthday party for Charles at Highgrove. They recruited showbusiness friends of the Royals, Stephen Fry and Emma Thompson, to help stage a skit in the style of the TV comedy *Blackadder* in which the boys also performed.

Earlier in 1998, only a little more than nine months after his mother's death, William had met his father's companion, Camilla Parker Bowles, for the first time.

Showing great maturity and sensitivity towards his father, William spent thirty minutes chatting to Camilla, the woman his mother had blamed for the break-up of her marriage. William realised how important Camilla is to Charles and that she makes him happy. Over tea and soft drinks at St James's Palace, they got to know each other, delighting a relieved Prince of Wales. Camilla attended the boys' fiftieth birthday party for their father.

During the Diana years, Charles had been portrayed as an uncaring and absentee father, while in reality he had always been loving and, in private, affectionate and demonstrative. But the Waleses' marriage breakdown and divorce, with all its ugliness, had torn the family apart and, to some extent, alienated young William from his family. He could not understand why his parents quarrelled and made each other so unhappy. Now Diana was no longer there and William, like his father and brother, had to rebuild his life – and Charles was to be the cornerstone. William and Harry accompanied the Prince of Wales to his 1998 Christmas staff party at The Ritz, in London's Piccadilly, close to their home at St James's Palace. The three Princes walked the short distance through Green Park to the plush party and looked very much a family unit, clinging closely together.

William's housemaster at Eton, Dr Gailey, and his wife, Shauna, with the Manor House dame, Miss Heathcote, were instrumental in seeing William through his time in the sixth form, along with his school friends, including chums from Ludgrove, like Andrew Charlton, John Richards and Harry Walsh. Friends of the family also rallied round and there were private holidays for William with the van Straubenzees in Cornwall, the Legge-Bourkes in Wales and the van Cutsems in Norfolk.

William's uncle Earl Spencer, Diana's brother Charles, who in his address at the Princess's funeral pledged to nurture her boys, visited William at Eton in June 1998 and invited him to Althorp House, the Spencers' stately home. William went to Althorp on 6 July – five days after what would have been his mother's thirty-seventh birthday – it is highly likely he visited Diana's unmarked grave on a small island situated in a lake in the grounds. Lord Spencer has spent much of his time abroad, particularly in South Africa, and has rarely had the opportunity to see William

and Harry in recent years.

In the summer of 1999, William learned to drive. A car can give a young person greater independence but for William it also satisfies his love of speed. Of course, with a police bodyguard sitting in the passenger seat or following behind in an unmarked car or people carrier, there is no scope for nudging the speed limit. Nevertheless William likes the thrill of driving.

William was introduced to motoring at an early age when, just before his fourth birthday, he was made the six-millionth member of the Automobile Association and given an AA life membership, so if his car breaks down, help is only a phone call away. Before he was old enough to drive on public roads, he went go-karting with his mother and was dashing around the private tracks of the Queen's Balmoral estate on a quad-bike.

He likes motorbikes and has passed his test, allowing him to ride without a learner's plate. He took Eton's sixth-form motorcycle maintenance course and in November 1998 went on a school visit to the Triumph factory at Hinckley, Leicestershire. Riding around the roads of the Cotswolds on a 125cc bike, anonymous in his motorcycle helmet and visor, was a liberation for sixteen-year-old William.

As soon as he was seventeen, the legal age to start driving a car on Britain's public roads, with an instructor, William began driving lessons. His seventeenth birthday present from his father was a second-hand Volkswagon Golf GTi in which he would learn to drive. The Prince applied for a provisional driving licence and was eager to take to the roads without delay.

A month later, William showed off his driving skills for the first time when he plucked up the courage to drive in front of the world's media at Highgrove. He successfully negotiated the gravel driveway of the Gloucestershire residence and managed to brake just in time, a few yards from a bank of TV cameras. Waiting on the doorstep were Prince Harry and the Prince of Wales who said of his eldest son's driving, 'He's going very well.' Although the heir to the throne admitted, 'I haven't actually had the experience of being driven by him.'

William chose to be pictured in a loaned car – a new, silver Ford Focus – to safeguard his privacy when he drives

his own car. The Prince was accompanied by Metropolitan Police driving instructor Sergeant Chris Gilbert who sat in the passenger seat. It is likely that as well as elementary road skills, required to pass his driving test, William was also being taught some advanced techniques to counter possible terrorist threats to his safety. Sergeant Gilbert, based at Scotland Yard's Hendon driving school in north-west London, had thirty years' experience as an instructor and examiner, including teaching anti-hijack and counter surveillance driving techniques.

Stepping from the car, with a broad grin on his face, 6ft-plus William towered over his father and brother. But Harry had also grown and was catching up with William and Charles, who is 5ft 9ins tall. As the proud father stood with his two sons either side of him, he joked, 'This is just to show how quickly I'm shrinking.'

William passed his driving test on 27 July 1999, just five weeks after his seventeenth birthday.

The following year, Prince William received an unusual eighteenth birthday present, an official coat of arms, authorised by the Queen. He helped design the crest, which incorporates an emblem from his mother's family arms. William's crest – a lion and unicorn, either side of a shield, topped by a coronet and second, smaller lion – features a small, red scallop from the Spencer coat of arms. The scallop appears four times on the middle point of four, three-pointed white collars, around the lions, unicorn and shield. The collars or labels, as they are called, can only be used in arms of the sovereign's children or the eldest son of the Prince of Wales. There is no motto.

Prince William still could not be persuaded to give a formal birthday interview that year. But he did agree to answer submitted questions and his responses revealed a modern young man trying to cope with his fame.

William said he liked casual clothes, dance and pop music, and driving his car. 'I enjoy dancing but don't go clubbing that often,' he said.

Team sports – water polo, football and rugby – were his forte. His spare time was spent with friends, going to the cinema to see action films, and watching football and rugby matches.

Revealingly, he said he would like to be a private person away from the public and media spotlight. 'I don't like the

attention. I feel uncomfortable with it,' he said. 'But I have particularly appreciated being left alone at Eton, which has allowed me to concentrate on my school work and enjoy being with my friends without being followed by cameras. I am grateful to the media for helping to protect my privacy and I hope I can enjoy the same freedom at university.'

Asked how he coped with the adulation of girls, he said, 'In my own way. Trying to explain might be counter-productive.'

Did he have a girlfriend? 'I like to keep my private life private,' he said, discreetly.

Asked about being linked with blonde American pop star Britney Spears, he said, 'There's been a lot of nonsense put about by PR companies. I don't like being exploited in this way but as I get older it's increasingly hard to prevent.'

He confirmed he was taking a year out after he left Eton and that he hoped to study history of art at university. But the teenage Prince, who was sitting A-level exams at the time of his birthday, was nervous about his results and would not say which university was his first choice. Clearly, he aimed to secure a university place on merit.

William said he would be studying on his birthday for an art history exam the following day and would celebrate his eighteenth later, privately with friends.

With the backing of his father, William planned to complete his full-time education before beginning solo royal duties. He had not yet made up his mind about a future career, perhaps in one of the armed services. 'At this stage I just want to get through university,' he said. 'I know there's been a lot of speculation but the truth is I haven't made up my mind yet.'

William agreed to be filmed at Eton to mark his eighteenth birthday – and bared his muscular torso on TV playing water polo.

He also revealed himself to be a keen chef, cooking chicken paella and chatting about the recipe. Wearing a butcher's apron over his prefect's uniform, he was filmed chopping the ingredients and frying them in a large pan. Not everything went to plan, as his friend, with whom he was preparing the meal, spilt some stock. 'Do something,'

As the proud father stood with his two sons, he joked, 'This is just to show how quickly I'm shrinking.'

William said, laughing, as things started going wrong.

The Prince chose a cookery course from around ninety options in an extensive general studies programme at the school. Working from recipes, William prepared dishes which pupils and masters then sampled. Other options available in general studies ranged from philosophy, the arts and languages to a course entitled 'The Troubles in Ulster'. But cookery was particularly popular and would come in handy when William was at university and catering for himself.

When the A-level results came through that summer, William had once again scored high marks – 'A' in geography, 'B' in history of art and 'C' in biology – which were good enough grades to assure him a place at the university of his choice. Speculation was rife that he would follow his father to Cambridge or perhaps opt for Oxford. But William's sights were set on Scotland and either Edinburgh University or St Andrews, the alma mater of housemaster Dr Gailey, who was a strong influence on the Prince. In June 1999 James Ogilvy, the son of Princess Alexandra and Sir Angus Ogilvy and cousin to William, had taken him and a friend on unofficial visits to both universities. William chose St Andrews, Scotland's oldest university, founded in 1411 on the east coast of Fife.

He decided to study for a four-year Bachelor of Arts degree in history of art, after all, his grandmother has many of the paintings he would study on her palace walls! In February 1999, during the school half-term, William had worked at Spinks, the London fine art dealers in St James's. The business attachment gave him an initial insight into the art world from the auction houses and great galleries to the restoration workshops of skilled craftsmen. Clearly the experience had inspired the Prince to pursue his interest in this field.

6

ROYAL SOAP

Old-fashioned deference has, to some extent, survived the social upheaval of the last century. William may agree with those who believe that the monarchy is part of the British psyche – something that people need rather than merely want. It seems that some people really do need a king, queen, prince or princess to look up to or to provide a welcome distraction in an otherwise humdrum existence.

Today, the world's fascination with the monarchy is fed by the media – from newspapers and magazines to television and the Internet, where official and unofficial websites abound to feed the habit of royalty junkies. For many of these people the lives of the Royals are no more than another gripping drama played out on their television screens, a never-ending soap opera laid on for their entertainment.

Indeed, with the seemingly unrelenting public interest in him, threatening to invade the privacy that every decent individual deserves, William must himself feel at times as if he is living in a soap opera. Ironically, the very thing that may make the monarchy popular with many people – a fascination with the rich and famous – is the aspect of the institution that William seems to dislike most. Despite his royal birthright, William wants a normal life and he remains an essentially private person. There is little doubt that he would prefer no fuss and no special attention.

Except for the unthinkable among members of the Royal Family – abdication or giving up his place in the line of succession – there is no escape for William. He was born to be king. Few children have their future decided so completely for them, without any real chance of self-determination.

When he was young, being told he would one day be king may have excited him but when he was old enough to understand the enormity of the lifetime's commitment, he was probably rightly unnerved. After all, being sovereign, with the expectations and personal restrictions imposed on a constitutional monarch, is a daunting and suffocating prospect. A ten-year-old William told his mother, 'When I grow up I want to be a policeman and look after you, Mummy.' His younger brother Harry put him straight. 'Oh no you can't, you've got to be king,' he said.

If the British monarchy is seen as an upper-class soap opera, then Prince William is a character who, for the time being, has been written out of the show. He makes

'There's been a lot of nonsense
put about by PR companies.
I don't like being exploited in
this way but as I get older it's
increasingly hard to prevent.'

occasional appearances but wishes to remain out of the limelight until the end of his university education. However, he is scripted to return as the nation's love interest and the Royal Family's tall and handsome saviour.

William and Harry's mother, Diana, was the classic royal soap star. Her death revealed the extent to which people empathised and identified with her emotional struggle. The fairy-tale Princess was a media icon, a Queen of Hearts and the People's Princess. Whether she was dazzling in the latest high-fashion gown or braving a minefield dressed in pedal-pushers, Diana was hot news. She was a sort of international celebrity whose marriage breakdown and infidelity, as well as the adultery of her husband, captivated a worldwide audience.

Diana's style lives on in her son William who, at twenty-one, is showing himself to be a popular and charismatic Prince. His mother was keen for William to know how all his future subjects lived, not just the privileged. When he was still a young boy she took him to meet the homeless and disadvantaged in emergency shelters, and to meet people with terminal illnesses, including AIDS, in hospitals and hospices.

'I want them to have an understanding of people's emotions, of people's insecurities, of people's distress, of their hopes and dreams,' the Princess once said of her sons.

The influence of Diana, not only on her son but also on the rest of the Royal Family, and the consequent evolution of the monarchy into a more populist institution, has contributed to William's character. What William thinks is expected of him and his perception of the institution he will one day head have also helped shape his identity. The combination of his private and public lives, as well as the constant tension created by this division, will undoubtedly influence who he is and how he feels about the world.

While mystique and dignity may be important factors in maintaining the monarchy's popularity, the former, at least, has been compromised by exposure in the media and a new more honest and open monarchy must surely emerge if it is to survive. William will inherit a different monarchy to that of his grandmother, indeed he is already part of a restructuring of the institution, and he will reign in different times. His father will make changes and adapt the monarchy to suit his era. William must also continue to

move with the times and he will have to prepare himself for a life in front of the cameras. Television soaps depend on good viewing figures, as does the twenty-first-century monarchy. They both have to be popular and relevant to survive. So, like it or not, William finds himself cast as a leading man in the royal drama and he must learn to play his part with care if he is to protect his public image.

Diana told *New Yorker* editor Tina Brown, shortly before she died, 'All my hopes are on William now. I try to drum it into him about the media – the dangers and how he must understand and handle it. It's too late for the rest of the family. But William, I think he has it.'

The Royal Family did indeed fall foul of the media, in October and November 2002, when 'what the butler saw' became an explosive episode of the royal saga. Diana's former butler Paul Burrell was acquitted of stealing more than 300 items from her estate, the Prince of Wales and William. The case collapsed after the controversial intervention of the Queen and the butler walked free from court to sell his story to a tabloid newspaper. Sensational revelations, sordid allegations, claims and counter-claims made daily headlines. William and Harry were forced to endure media speculation about their mother's role in this damaging deluge of criticisms of both the Windsors and the Spencers.

For William the news stories must have been an unpleasant reminder of the darker side to his mother's difficult life. Not only had he endured the pain of his parents' unhappy marriage and Diana's early death, he now had to re-live the memories of those tragic times. Not for the first time, he was subjected to a post mortem of his mother's character. It was probably no less disturbing to witness doubts expressed over his grandmother, the Queen's, motives for a last-minute intervention in the Burrell case. Once again, the media was turning his life into a soap opera for the entertainment of the world.

'All my hopes are on William now. I try to drum it into him about the media – the dangers and how he must understand and handle it. It's too late for the rest of the family. But William, I think he has it.'

Diana told *New Yorker* editor Tina Brown, June 1997

'When I grow up I want to be a policeman and look after you, Mummy.' His younger brother Harry put him straight. 'Oh no you can't, you've got to be king,' he said.

7

GAP YEAR

After leaving Eton at the end of June 2000, William embarked on a 'gap year' before starting university. Dismissing the temptation to play polo for twelve months, he was determined to do something useful and constructive with his year off from studying. After discussing possible options with his friends and family, William decided to travel.

First stop was Belize, in central America, where he joined the Welsh Guards on a gruelling jungle survival course. For four days he trekked through a jungle alive with deadly snakes, scorpions, spiders and crocodiles. He learned how to live off the land and had to kill a chicken for food, helping to wring the bird's neck and hack off its head before plucking it. The jungles of Belize, a former British colony, are also home to gangs of rogue soldiers and kidnappers. But William was well protected, surrounded by 140 troops and accompanied by police bodyguards as well as two elite SAS soldiers. This was character-building stuff, nevertheless, and it was only the start of an action-packed gap year.

A study break on the faraway island of Rodrigues, near Mauritius, in the Indian Ocean came shortly afterwards. There William spent a month on a Royal Geographical Society research project named Shoals of Capricorn. The programme's aim was to advise on ways of managing and protecting the area from environmental damage. William helped survey the coral reefs, his work involving snorkelling and scuba diving. By the time he returned to England his skin was tanned and his fair hair bleached blond by the sun and sea.

Back at Highgrove, William agreed to face the press. Looking ruggedly handsome in jeans, jumper and trainers, he answered questions about the next stage of his gap year and, with his father at his side lending moral support, also addressed a more difficult issue. His mother's former private secretary, Patrick Jephson, had written a controversial book about his time working for the Princess and William had agreed to say something about this, albeit in response to a planted question from a 'friendly' journalist. His brow furrowed and his smile disappeared but he spoke without rancour: 'Of course Harry and I are both upset about it, that our mother's trust has been betrayed and even now she is being exploited. But I don't

really want to say any more about it.'

It was a mature eighteen-year-old who faced the world's media, defending his mother's memory and putting aside his own dislike of publicity. William had seen the way his mother had both courted the cameras and then tried to hide from them. He had seen the way the cameras had sometimes made her cry. It should be no surprise, therefore, that he is reluctant to enter the limelight and feels uncomfortable with media attention. But, with coaching and encouragement from his father, the superstar Prince is slowly coming to terms with his future life in the focus of a camera lens.

Of his gap year, William revealed he was about to leave for Chile, in South America, where he would join a ten-week Raleigh International expedition. By playing sponsored water polo, he had raised enough money to finance most of the trip – his father chipped in – and also pay for a disadvantaged youngster to take part. Good public relations, a cynic might say, but in truth a sign of William's social conscience, so carefully nurtured by his mother and latterly by his father. 'Basically, I wanted to do something constructive with my gap year,' said William. 'I thought this was a way of trying to help people out and meeting a whole range of people from other countries, and at the same time helping people in remote areas of Chile.'

The trip to Patagonia in southern Chile turned out to be a memorable experience for a teenage Prince who had already accumulated many memories in his eighteen years. The youngster training to be king lived in a shack, slept in a tent, chopped logs, cooked meals, scrubbed floors and even cleaned a communal toilet. He entertained children, joined in their games and took a turn as a DJ, playing music in a tin-shack nightclub in the remote village of Caleta Tortel.

'The living conditions here aren't exactly what I'm used to . . .' he said at the time. 'You don't have any secrets. You share everything with everyone. I found it very difficult myself to start with because I am a very private person. But I learnt to deal with it.'

William worked alongside 110 other young volunteers from varied backgrounds on environmental and community projects, including improving local buildings and constructing walkways. Heavy work, but William

was a fit teenager with a well-developed physique through years of playing sport. He assisted with map-making and tracking rare species of deer, providing valuable data for nature conservationists. In addition, the action-man Prince, a description also given to his father when Charles was younger, went trekking in the snow-covered hills of the region.

'He's really laid-back and easy-going,' said one of the expedition leaders. 'He gets on well with absolutely everybody, whatever their backgrounds. He gets stuck in and has a good laugh. He has earned the respect of the venturers and staff, and is very well liked. He's not popular because of who he happens to be. He's popular because of who he is as a person. He's popular on his own merit. He gets on with the work, he's very humble and likes to be normal, and there's no reference to his background. He's a very comfortable person, a very genuine person, very open and honest, and he puts everyone at ease. If there are tensions, he's the sort of person who will make a joke and it all settles down again. He's a real peacemaker among the group if it's needed. His star quality is that he's just completely human and normal and one of the gang.'

William returned home for Christmas and during January and February 2001 worked on a dairy farm in the southwest of England, just before the devastating outbreak of foot-and-mouth disease hit Britain. Surprisingly, the thing he enjoyed most during his gap year was working as a farm labourer – at the minimum wage – rising before dawn to milk cows and muck out.

The final leg of his pre-university gap year was spent in Africa where, for more than three months, he travelled through several countries on safari, involving himself with game conservation.

William did not attend Freshers' Week at St Andrews University, the traditional settling-in week for new students, which in a town with twenty-two pubs – more per square mile than any other British university town – tends to be a boozy affair. 'It would have been a media frenzy and that's not fair on the other students,' he told the Press Association, continuing with surprising frankness, 'plus I thought I would probably end up in the gutter, completely wrecked, and the people I had met that week wouldn't end up being my friends anyway. It also meant another week's holiday.'

'The living conditions here aren't exactly what I'm used to . . . You don't have any secrets. You share everything with everyone. I found it very difficult myself to start with because I am a very private person. But I learnt to deal with it.'

William disclosed that he planned to drive to Edinburgh, an hour away by car, for evenings out if the St Andrews night-life did not measure up. 'Weekends at St Andrews are not particularly vibrant. I'm not a party animal, but I like to go out sometimes like anyone else,' he explained.

He laughed off reports that some girls at St Andrews wanted to bag him as a husband. 'I suppose they're saying that tongue-in-cheek,' he said. 'But people who try to take advantage and get a piece of me – I spot it quickly and soon go off them. I just want to go to university and have fun. I want to be an ordinary student. I mean, it's not like I'm getting married – though that's how it feels sometimes. It will get easier as time goes on. Everyone will get bored of me, which they do.'

The Prince said he hoped to make a broad cross-section of friends at university and not just stay with the ex-public school types, known as 'yahs', who make up sixty per cent of St Andrews' 6,500 students. 'It's not as if I choose my friends on the basis of where they are from or what they are,' he said. 'It's about their character and who they are and whether we get on. I just hope I can meet people I get on with. I don't care about backgrounds.'

William expected lively debates with anti-monarchists while at university. 'To me, someone can hold a view about something without it making a difference to who they are. Everyone has opinions and they are entitled to them. I can still get on with them, even if I don't agree with what they might believe.'

Like most new university students, William thought that he would miss home but was looking forward to greater freedom. 'Having more independence is quite a big thing, although I've always got policemen around so I'm never completely independent. But I'm looking forward to being able to manage my own time in a relaxed atmosphere.'

Explaining how St Andrews, famous as the home of golf, won his heart, he said, 'I didn't want to go to an English university because I have lived there and wanted to try somewhere else. I also knew I would be seeing a lot of Wales in the future. I do love Scotland. There is plenty of space. I love the hills and I thought St Andrews had a community feel to it. I've never lived near the sea so it will

be very different. In St Andrews, it's a small community
and so I can mingle. Edinburgh is just too big and busy.'

Before actually arriving at university, William carried
out a number of official engagements in Scotland and
showed his increasing confidence and expertise at working
a crowd. He moved effortlessly between adoring pensioners
and crowds of screaming teenagers. His charm brought
back memories of his mother, Diana. Seasoned royal
watchers commented that the undergraduate Prince had at
last come of age.

Accompanying his father, he visited Sighthill, a
deprived Glasgow housing estate, Paisley and Edinburgh
where, at the US Consulate, he signed a book of
condolence for those affected by the 11 September terrorist
attacks in America. 'With deepest sympathy. Love from
William,' he wrote. Later, he said, 'I wanted to let them
know they are not forgotten and that people do care about
them. It was such a serious loss of life.' William revealed
how he had watched the news reports of the terrorist
attacks on New York and Washington in stunned horror.
He had been out the night before, was staying with friends
and sleeping in late when the news broke in Britain at
around 2 p.m. He said, 'Suddenly, there was panic in the
house and everyone was rushing to watch the television. I
just watched the news and sat there in stunned silence for
ages. No one said anything.' His father signed the
condolence book: 'With heartfelt condolences to the loved
ones of all those who died so tragically in New York.'

anything to go by, William does indeed have varied tastes. From his seat in the front row of the Royal Box, he applauded – albeit with varying degrees of enthusiasm – everything from Latino Ricky Martin, S Club 7, Mis-teeq, Atomic Kitten, Annie Lennox, Bryan Adams, Will Young, Blue, The Corrs, Brian May and Queen, Toploader and Emma Bunton to crooner Tony Bennett, the evergreen Tom Jones, veteran Sir Cliff Richard and Welsh diva Dame Shirley Bassey, a favourite of his grandfather, the Duke of Edinburgh.

But heavy-metal rocker Ozzy Osbourne was clearly a royal favourite, rousing William with the Black Sabbath anthem 'Paranoid'. Phil Collins, who does good work for the Prince of Wales's Prince's Trust charity, had William clapping along, as did ex-Beach Boy Brian Wilson with the surfing hit 'Good Vibrations'.

William was sitting in a group with his brother and cousins Princesses Beatrice and Eugenie, and Peter and Zara Phillips and the young Royals could not help chuckling at Prime Minister's wife Cherie Blair who lost herself singing and clapping.

Years ago, a young William admitted to having a crush on Baby Spice Emma Bunton and, at the end of her version of The Supremes' classic 'Baby Love', she risked embarrassing him with, 'Here's a big kiss for Wills.' Atomic Kitten's Liz McClarnon, who said she was smitten by William, had hoped to get to know him and, after the show, he chatted with the girl band, seemingly not noticing their skimpy dresses.

William's pedigree as a pop pundit is almost as impressive as his royal roots. He knows the old songs as well as the new. He appreciated the class of rock's royalty, Eric Clapton, Steve Winwood, Ray Davies, Rod Stewart, Joe Cocker and former Beatle Sir Paul McCartney. At sixteen, he was heavily into techno house music and his father complained of the pulsating bass beat belting out and thudding through Highgrove, his stately residence where Mozart's sonatas might be more at home. But William, who taught the Queen Mother to mimic Ali G, also likes hip hop. Chatting to S Club's Bradley McIntosh after the Palace pop concert, the Prince said he was switched on to the controversial rapper Eminem. 'He told me he was a really big Eminem fan,' said Bradley. 'He recommended The

Eminem Show album and said he was playing it in his car
all the time. I can't wait until William's king. Then I can
meet him and say "Yo bro. How's it going?"'

William began his second academic year at university by
moving into a flat with friends in one of the town's most
elegant Georgian streets. One of his flatmates, Kate
Middleton, hit the headlines for her daring display at a
saucy students' charity fashion show. William paid £200 for
a VIP seat to see the 'undies parade' in which his dark-
haired friend Kate sashayed along the catwalk in a see-
through black lace dress, revealing her underwear. William
and Kate have much in common – they are the same age,
both love sport, study art history and spent a gap year in
Chile – but friends said they were not romantically linked.
Fellow Old Etonian Fergus Boyd was William and Kate's
choice as a third flatmate. A police bodyguard also lives in
the flat and between them they share the above-average rent.

A mountain bike seems to be the favoured means of
transport for William around the cobbled streets of St
Andrews. He can be seen peddling to lectures as if there was
not a moment to spare. The Prince said he wanted to keep
himself to himself at university, but he still likes to go out
and lead as normal a life as possible. He indulges his sweet
tooth and has been seen in a local sweet shop and hovering
around the pick'n'mix counter in the town's Woolworths. To
relax he frequents some of the St Andrews bars, including
the up-market Ma Bells on the Scores as well as The Gin
House in South Street and Broons in North Street.

William has joined the university water polo club and
usually plays on Thursday evenings. On Wednesday
afternoons, set aside for sport, he works out for a couple of
hours in the university gym. Last year, he played rugby and
Sunday league football for St Salvator's Hall and, according
to other players, kept up a good standard. He told a guest at
an Edinburgh royal garden party that he had also taken up
water-skiing.

Despite persistent reports to the contrary, William does
not smoke. Like most boys, he tried a cigarette when he was
younger but did not like it. To his father's relief – Charles
hates smoking – William is a confirmed non-smoker.

Style-watchers may have noticed that William does not
wear a watch or signet ring like other men in the Royal
Family. Ironically, the only jewellery the young man

and daring to breakaway from Palace rules but owes a lot to Charles's solid sense of quality and good taste.

Being a modern Prince, influenced by new styles, his hair has been through changes. There was the boyish long fringe, behind which he liked to hide with his head bowed. Then, at Eton, he graduated to a slightly shorter but tousled look. At university, where he is known to be a somewhat late riser, he adopts the just-out-of-bed, slept-in look. Fortunately for William, rushing to a morning lecture, it is cool to look a little dishevelled.

Prince William may be camera-shy but, without doubt, he is a pin-up idol for millions of teenage girls around the world.

The emergence of William as a teen heart-throb came as long ago as October 1995 when *Smash Hits*, the British pop music magazine, published a poster of him. Even dressed in a school blazer, grey trousers, collar and tie, he was an instant hit with the girls and the magazine quickly sold out. William was good for sales.

Lovesick girls started writing to him, sending their photographs and trinkets, and on St Valentine's Day he received fifty-four cards. The following year, William's postbag had grown to 500 Valentine cards and thereafter to more than 1,000. A magazine gave away 250,000 'I Love Willy' stickers, the editor enthusing that William was classic boyfriend material.

With his blue eyes, blond hair and warm smile, William was the focus of female desire in November 1997 when he attended a VIP lunch at the Royal Naval College in Greenwich, south-east London, to celebrate the Queen and the Duke of Edinburgh's fiftieth wedding anniversary. Some 600 screaming teenagers greeted him, to the surprise of organisers, the police and lunch guests, including modest William.

However, his first real taste of adulation came in March 1998 when the teenage girls of Canada gave William a pop star's welcome. They besieged his luxury hotel in Vancouver, screamed, swooned, burst into tears and then pursued him to the Rocky Mountain ski slopes.

Just six months after his mother's funeral, when he walked behind her coffin in a solemn cortège and broke the hearts of people throughout the world, William had inherited Diana's celebrity mantle. These were unprecedented scenes. No other male member of the Royal Family had ever been given such a reception. 'Willsmania' had arrived.

He was in British Columbia, on Canada's scenic west coast, with his father and brother. The three Princes were carrying out official engagements in and around Vancouver before heading off for a private skiing holiday in the popular resort of Whistler. William stole the show. Teenage girls mobbed him. They tried to pull at his clothes and hair, and they held up posters saying, 'William It's Me You're Looking For', 'We Love You William', 'I'm Yours'.

With his blue eyes,
blond hair and warm
smile, William was the
focus of female desire ...

At first William seemed uncomfortable but gradually he relaxed and could even deal with his younger brother's friendly taunts. Harry's turn as a teen idol was yet to come.

Perhaps the defining moment of the visit came just before the Princes were due to depart by helicopter from the Vancouver waterfront bound for Whistler. William and Harry were presented with 'Roots' designer jackets and flat caps. Without hesitation, William took off his suit jacket and slipped into his cool new outfit, putting the cap on back-to-front, then twirled and gave a rap-style roll of the wrist and shoulders.

His father and brother looked on in awe and admiration. Here was a superstar in the making – a super-royal.

When the girls calmed down enough to speak, they said William was 'gorgeous' but it was clear they also admired the courage he displayed after his mother's death. Some felt maternal towards him.

As soon as the Princes left for Whistler, William's die-hard fans followed, turning up, skimpily dressed, on the frozen ski slopes to swoon again at their handsome royal idol.

Polo, like skiing, is a glamorous sport and attracts beautiful women looking for rich husbands. William, who is passionate about polo, has already been pictured at swanky venues in the company of attentive young women hoping to get their name and number in the Prince's little black book. But the polo pretties will have to compete with girls at William's university where applications, particularly from Americans wanting to meet a Prince, rocketed by forty-four per cent when he signed up in September 2001.

Their country's republican roots clearly count as naught to American teenage girls when there is a Prince on campus. The British Council in Washington reported an avalanche of inquiries about studying at Scotland's oldest university. History tutors at St Andrews will no doubt point out that the last British monarch – Edward VIII – to fall for an American woman – divorcee Wallis Simpson – lost his job.

Thousands of girls clamoured to study alongside William on his history of art course. In fact, eight out of ten students on the Prince's course are women. Perhaps they had been told that a third of all St Andrews' students meet their spouses while studying there.

When William enrolled at the university, which is nicknamed 'St Randy's' because of its reputation for wild

parties, more than 4,000 fans packed the streets of the small Fife town to see him arrive. Scores of girls screamed themselves hoarse. And he had received an equally rapturous reception during a whistle-stop tour of Scotland before arriving at St Andrews.

A group of four teenage girls, who had travelled from Edinburgh to Fife to see William, squealed with delight when he coyly waved at them. Kirsten Taylor, fifteen, said, 'We just wanted to see what he looked like in real life, and he's so beautiful. I think I know where we'll be spending some of our weekends in the future.'

Female students at St Andrews have devised a way of 'Wills spotting'. The girls keep each other up to date with his movements by text messaging on their mobile phones.

William likes to dance but he uses his fastest footwork when asked about girlfriends. He knows there is intense interest in his love life and he is determined to keep the identity of his dates strictly confidential. Of course, he has to be careful about whom he chooses to see. Pick the wrong girl and she may run to the Sunday newspapers and 'kiss and tell'. Not only would it be cringingly embarrassing, it would also be undignified if such intimate details of William's private life were so unfairly disclosed.

The Prince has to choose his friends well. He has to be sure that they want to know him because of what he is like not who he is. Many of his friends come from aristocratic backgrounds, familiar with the unwritten protocol of how to behave. So far, William has been a good judge of character and chosen well, sensing when a person is genuine and worth knowing, regardless of their background.

When it comes to girlfriends, he has plenty of hopefuls to choose from. He is royal, rich, handsome and charming, not to mention well-educated and unassuming. In short, he is one of the world's most eligible bachelors. And girls literally throw themselves at him.

William started out preferring blondes. Boyhood infatuations included Pamela Anderson, of TV's *Baywatch*, and supermodels Cindy Crawford and Claudia Schiffer. His mother teased him about Cindy and even arranged for her to come to Kensington Palace, in April 1996, as a treat for her adolescent son. Cindy also sent William signed photographs. Later that year, Diana fixed William a date, at their palace home, with Claudia, as well as catwalk stars Naomi

months when he phoned her parents' home near Tiverton in Devon to invite her on the Aegean cruise. They were introduced by a mutual friend and she obviously made a big impression on the Prince. Since their holiday together, William has invited Emilia, who was a boarder at the exclusive Marlborough College, Wiltshire, to a royal shooting party on his father's Duchy of Cornwall estate. However, she has also been spotted in the company of William's younger brother, Harry, at a polo match in Cowdray Park, West Sussex.

Emilia's mother, Elizabeth, who is the sister of the tenth Viscount Exmouth and a regional director of Sotheby's auction house, said at the time of the cruise that William was 'a lucky young man' to have the company of the girls. But she added, 'Emilia is very lucky, I wish it was me!'

Also invited aboard the 'love boat' was Emilia's friend Mary Forestier-Walker, as well as Laura Fellowes, daughter of Diana's sister Jane, and Laura Parker Bowles, daughter of the Prince of Wales's partner, Camilla Parker Bowles.

William and his cruise companions were chaperoned by his father and Camilla along with an eclectic mix of guests sharing the luxury of the 400ft MV *Alexander*, which boasts ten state rooms, disco and ballroom, swimming pool and helicopter – and manages to stay afloat despite 300 tonnes of marble fittings.

Other girls in William's elite social circle have included the Honourable Alexandra Knatchbull, daughter of Lord and Lady Romsey; Lady Rosanagh Innes-Ker, daughter of the Duke of Roxburgh; and recently knighted airline tycoon Sir Richard Branson's daughter, Holly.

The Prince clearly has an eye for the girls and while he was in Chile during his gap year, he noticed a pretty nursery worker and danced the night away with her at a disco. Monica Barra Godoy, at twenty-two four years older than William, danced with him in a nightclub in the remote Patagonian village of Caleta Tortel while he was a Raleigh International volunteer.

Describing the incident, friend Alejandra Zurita said, 'A band was playing and the Raleigh volunteers, including William, had been drinking a local spirit called Pisco. They all seemed very merry and in the party mood. Monica danced with William several times to a mixture of salsa and rock music. It was always she who invited him onto the dance floor, but he didn't hold back. He looked very happy.'

'Willsmania' had arrived. William stole the show. Teenage girls mobbed him. They tried to pull at his clothes and hair, and they held up posters saying, 'William It's Me You're Looking For', 'We Love You William', 'I'm Yours'.

Vancouver, March 1998

of the monarchy or its modernised version, will depend
crucially on how he untangles the confused feelings that his
mother and father's aggravated relationship must have
produced in him.

William has experienced a wide range of situations and
lifestyles that should allow him to better understand his
future subjects. Diana's bequest to William was to get in
touch with the people. He is the natural heir to his mother's
style. It remains to be seen how far William's genuine aims
to fit in, to empathise with and relate to the wider public,
will make a real difference.

In an increasingly egalitarian climate, the monarchy has
faced – and survived – repeated crises which republican
pundits predicted would bring down the House of Windsor.
The fallout from the Burrell case rained down bad publicity
on the Royals, causing great damage that will take time to
repair. Few senior Royals, not even the Queen, were left
untainted by the acrid slurs and allegations.

Prince William's reputation, however, emerged unscathed
from this royal drama. If anything he could be seen as a
victim of the trial. After the collapse of the case against Mr
Burrell, police officers were accused of having misled
William and Charles about the strength of evidence against
the butler. The Princes would have preferred to see no
criminal charges brought against the former royal servant.
For them, the resulting unsuccessful prosecution dredged up
the past and cast a shadow over the future.

After their attempted damage control following the
Burrell case, the Royal Family and their advisers must tread
carefully. Debate on the nature and scope of the monarchy
is likely to continue, erupting every time a Royal puts a foot
wrong. But William's copybook remains unblotted and while
his popular image as a handsome young Prince in touch
with the people provides the royal soap opera with a genuine
hero, William remains the monarchy's hope and future.